THE STATE OF THE WORLD'S CHILDREN
1992

Oxford University Press, Walton Street, Oxford
OX2 6DP, Oxfordshire, U.K.
Oxford, New York, Toronto, Delhi, Bombay, Calcutta,
Madras, Karachi, Peealing Jaya, Singapore, Hong Kong,
Tokyo, Nairobi, Dar-es-Salaam, Cape Town, Melbourne,
Auckland and associated companies in Beirut, Berlin,
Ibadan, Nicosia.

Oxford is a trade mark of Oxford University Press
Published in the United States by Oxford University
Press, New York.

Any part of The State of the World's Children may be
freely reproduced with the appropriate acknowledgement.

British Library Cataloguing in Publication Data
The state of the world's children 1992
1. Children - Care and hygiene
613' 0432 RJ101
ISBN 0-19-262228-5

ISSN 0265-718X

The Library of Congress has catalogued this serial
publication as follows:-
The state of the world's children - Oxford
New York: Oxford University Press for UNICEF v.:ill.;
20cm. Annual. Began publication in 1980.
1. Children - Developing countries - Periodicals.
2. Children - Care and hygiene - Developing countries -
Periodicals. I. UNICEF.
HQ 792.2.S73 83-647550 362.7' 1'091724

UNICEF, UNICEF House, 3 U.N. Plaza, New York,
N.Y. 10017 U.S.A.
UNICEF, Palais des Nations, CH. 1211
Geneva 10, Switzerland.

Cover and design: Miller, Craig and Cocking, Woodstock, U.K.
Charts: Stephen Hawkins, Oxford, U.K.
Typesetting: Duncan Carr Desktop Publishing, Wallingford, U.K.
Printing: Burgess & Son (Abingdon) Ltd., U.K.

Edited and produced for UNICEF and Oxford University
Press by P & L Adamson, 18 Observatory Close,
Benson, Wallingford, Oxon OX10 6NU, U.K.
tel 0491-38431, fax 0491-25426

THE STATE
OF THE WORLD'S
CHILDREN
1992

James P. Grant
Executive Director of the
United Nations Children's Fund
(UNICEF)

PUBLISHED FOR UNICEF

Oxford University Press

CONTENTS

THE STATE OF THE WORLD'S CHILDREN 1992

PANELS

TEXT FIGURES

SUMMARY OF ISSUES

The political and economic changes of the last three years have made it clear that a new world order is emerging. This year's State of the World's Children report seeks to contribute to the agenda of that new order from the perspective of a worldwide organization which comes into daily contact with some of the greatest failings of the old.

The report puts forward 10 specific propositions:

1 That the promise of the World Summit for Children should be kept and that a new world order should bring an end to malnutrition, preventable disease, and illiteracy among so many millions of the world's children.

Fact: *A quarter of a million young children die every week; millions more live on with malnutrition and almost permanent ill health. Approximately half of all cases of malnutrition, disease, and early death are caused by five or six specific illnesses which can now be prevented or treated at very low cost.*

2 That the principle of 'first call for children' - meaning that protection for the growing bodies and minds of the young ought to have a first call on societies' resources - should become an accepted ethic of a new world order.

Fact: *In many nations of the developing world, the lack of this principle has meant that the debt crisis of the 1980s has been translated into rising levels of child malnutrition and falling levels of school enrolment. In many nations of the industrialized world, the lack of this same principle has meant that the rising affluence of the 1980s has been accompanied by a sharp increase in the proportion of children living in poverty.*

3 That if the issues of malnutrition, preventable disease, and widespread illiteracy are not confronted as a new world order evolves, then it will be very much more difficult to reduce the rate of population growth and make the transition to environmentally sustainable development.

Fact: *Reducing child deaths gives parents more confidence in family planning. Most of the developing nations are now entering or approaching the stage at which further declines in child deaths are associated with much steeper declines in birth-rates. Doing what can now be done to protect the health and save the lives of millions of children will therefore help, not hinder, efforts to slow population growth.*

4 That the growing consensus around the importance of market economic policies should be accompanied by a corresponding consensus on the responsibility of governments to guarantee basic investments in people.

Fact: *On average, only about 12% of government spending in the developing world is devoted to basic investments such as primary health care and primary education for the poor majority.*

5 That increases in international aid should be based on a sustained and measurable commitment to meeting minimum human needs and for maintaining, in difficult times, the principle of a first call for children.

Fact: *Less than 10% of all aid is allocated to meeting the basic needs of the poor for health, primary education, clean water supply, and family planning.*

6 That international action on debt, aid, and trade should create an environment in which economic reform in the developing world can succeed in allowing its people to earn a decent living.

Fact: *The continuing debt crisis means that the poor world is now transferring $50 billion a year to the rich nations. Protectionism in the rich world costs the poor world a further $50 billion a year in lost exports.*

7 That a process of demilitarization should begin in the developing world and that, in step with that process, falling military expenditures in the industrialized nations should be linked to significant increases in international aid for development and for the resolution of common global problems.

Fact: *The amount now spent on the world's military exceeds the combined annual incomes of the poorest half of humanity. The goals of the World Summit for Children   including drastic reductions in malnutrition and disease and a basic education for all children - could be met by reallocating 10% of military expenditure in the developing world and 1% in the industrialized world.*

8 That the chains of Africa's debt be struck off and that the continent be given sufficient external support to allow internal reform to succeed in regenerating the momentum of development.

Fact: *Africa today is only managing to pay about one third of the interest due on its debts. Even this is absorbing a quarter of all its export earnings and costing the continent, each year, more than its total spending on the health and education of its people.*

9 That a new world order should oppose the apartheid of gender as vigorously as the apartheid of race.

Fact: *More than a million girls die each year simply because they are born female; the cause of death is the disease of discrimination.*

10 That the responsible planning of births is one of the most effective and least expensive ways of improving the quality of life on earth - both now and in the future - and that one of the greatest mistakes of our times is the failure to realise that potential.

Fact: *Over 50,000 illegal abortions are performed each day. Several million children die each year because they were born too soon after a previous birth or because they were born to mothers who were too young to give birth safely. Over 100,000 young women die every year because they do not have the knowledge or the means or the right to plan the number and spacing of their pregnancies. If all women could exercise that right, the rate of population growth would fall by approximately 30%.*

I
THE STATE OF THE WORLD'S CHILDREN 1992

James P. Grant

Agenda for a new order

Keeping the promise

First call for children

Fewer deaths, fewer births

Investing in people

Aid and need

The economic environment

Disarmament

Setting Africa free

The apartheid of gender

Planning births

The under-five mortality rate (U5MR) is the number of children who die before the age of five for every 1,000 live births. It is one of the principal indicators used by UNICEF to measure levels of, and changes in, the well-being of children. The U5MR also governs the order in which countries are listed in the statistical tables annexed to the *State of the World's Children* report.

Figures given for the U5MR of particular countries, in both the text and statistical tables, are derived from data produced by the United Nations Population Division and the United Nations Statistical Office.

For most developing countries, estimates of under-five deaths are derived from periodic household surveys rather than from the comprehensive civil registration systems used in industrialized countries. The latest U5MR estimates for developing countries are based on surveys for which the data was collected in 1987-88. These surveys reflect the actual situation in the mid 1980s. The 1990 U5MR estimates which appear in the statistical tables of this report are the result of extrapolating these data on the basis of trends in the early 1980s or earlier. Any change in the trend during the second half of the 1980s (resulting from, for example, the reaching of the 80% immunization target, the spread of oral rehydration therapy, or the increasing prevalence of AIDS) is therefore not reflected in the 1990 under-five mortality estimates. This also explains why the U5MR data given in the statistical tables (which must be based on internationally comparable data), may differ from individual (and possibly more recent) national estimates. Efforts are now being made to provide more recent estimates of under-five death mortality rates for all countries.

Agenda for a new order

This report is issued at a time when the world order which has dominated the political and economic life of the 20th century is visibly dying. It is offered, from the particular perspective of UNICEF's experience in working with some of humanity's most acute problems, as a contribution to the debate on the new world order which is struggling to be born.

In the blink of an historical eye, the world has witnessed the beginning of the end for apartheid, the liberation of Central and Eastern Europe, the ending of the 40-year cold war, the beginning of significant reductions in arms expenditures, the virtual abandonment of the idea of state economic monopoly, the narrowing of ideological divides, the strengthening of the economic heartbeat of Asia, the turn away from dictatorship in virtually every republic of Latin America, and a new impulse towards democracy, pluralism, and economic reform in Africa.

The period of history that is most difficult to understand is always one's own, but the suddenness and scale of these changes, in a landscape previously considered glacial in its rate of progress, suggests that we are

living through a revolution. If so, it is a revolution significantly different from revolutions past. It is different, first of all, in that its principal agent is not violence but communication. And as ends are often inherent in means, it is also different in that it is a revolution which appears to be transferring power not to the few but to the many.

These are profound differences in the process of historical change, differences which give a new meaning to the idea of the communications revolution. For in the many countries where political and economic change is now unfolding, it is the power of communication that is allowing the judgements, provoking the comparisons, heightening the frustrations and posing the alternatives. After years of somewhat empty talk about the global village, it is as if the first village meeting were being held and people were voting almost unanimously to reject the political and economic autocracies which have deprived them of choice without meeting their needs.

There have been unpleasant reminders of the vulnerability of this process of change, but recent events in the Soviet Union, and particularly on the streets of Moscow and St. Petersburg in August of 1991, have sent a message of courage to peoples all over the world. In many capital cities today, there is an almost tangible sense that some vital balance may be shifting, that the contours of the possible may be changing, that people are finding a new confidence in their own rights and abilities to participate in the management of their own affairs. And it may also be, although it should be said only tentatively, that there is a new nervousness, a new hesitancy, among those who might be tempted to suppress those rights.

This advance for democracy is not exclusively led by, or confined to, Eastern and Central Europe. Ten years ago, most of the 22 republics of Central and South America were gripped by dictatorships; today, all but one have an elected government. It also appears that Africa may now be embarked on a gradual political transformation. The shock waves from Eastern Europe and the Soviet Union are reverberating through that continent with a particular resonance because they are coinciding with the sudden and painful realization of the moral and financial inadequacies of many of its existing economic and political systems. Simultaneously, the ending of the cold war is raising new hopes that the destinies of many nations in Africa, and in other parts of the developing world, may now be detached from the superpower rivalries which have so distorted international relationships in the post-war era. Those rivalries have had much to do with the over-militarization of the developing world and with the perpetuation of the kind of regimes which, in so many countries and for so many decades, have denied human rights and crushed human hopes.

Despite an international agenda that is crowded with pressing political, economic, and environmental problems, there is therefore more cause for hope on the human horizon than perhaps at any other time in this century. It may be that the years ahead will show such optimism not to have been justified; but what is not in doubt is that a new order is emerging in our times.

A new order for children

This report seeks to contribute to the agenda of that new order from the perspective of a worldwide organization which comes into daily contact with some of the greatest failings of the old.

Those failings were the central issue of the *World Summit for Children* held in late September of 1990 at the United Nations headquarters in New York. The timing of the *Summit*, which brought together 159 nations, more than 70 of them represented by their Presidents or Prime Ministers, could not have been more propitious. The outcome - an agreed programme for, among other things, ending mass malnutrition, preventable disease, and widespread illiteracy before the end of the decade - amounted to a detailed description of a new order for the world's children (panel 1). The emergence of this agreement, at a time when the existing world order is rapidly changing, means that there is today a better chance than ever before of finding a place on the world's political agenda for the rights of children and for meeting the minimum needs of all families.

It is therefore obligatory, at this time, for all individuals and organizations charged with responsibility for such issues to enter as fully as possible into the debates that lie ahead. For a new page in world history is being turned, and if the needs of the poorest quarter of mankind, and of the children who are the most vulnerable of all, are again relegated to the footnotes of that page, then the new world order which is written there will be neither worthy of its times nor capable of meeting the challenges of the future.

Amid the many voices and the many clamorous issues that will compete for priority in the debates to come, this year's *State of the World's Children* report is therefore a plea for the inclusion of the issues which tend to be ignored and the voices which are normally silent. It is a plea, particularly, for the inclusion of those voices silenced by poverty and illiteracy, for those who are silenced by the effects of malnutrition and preventable disease, for those who are silenced by being born female, and for those many millions who are silenced by death almost before their lives have begun.

Specifically, the report submits 10 propositions for the consideration of all those - be they heads of state or members of the public - who are concerned to become involved in the discussion of the new world order which will evolve over the next few years. Taken together, they add up to a proposal that ending the absolute poverty of one quarter of mankind - the more than one billion people who still live and die with preventable hunger, disease, and illiteracy - should rank alongside the issues of preserving the peace and protecting the environment as priority items on the agenda of that new world order.

Contrary to widely held opinion, this great cause is far from being hopeless. We have already travelled three quarters of the way towards a world in which every man, woman, and child has adequate food, clean water, basic health care, and at least a primary education. And there is no technological or financial barrier to prevent the completion of that journey in our times.

Reaching these age-old goals is not a discrete cause and does not stand as a distraction from the new challenges of our times. Creating the conditions in which people can meet their own and their families needs for adequate nutrition, health care and education is an essential underpinning of efforts to meet those new challenges. As that investment liberates people's productivity, so it helps to stimulate economic growth; as it includes rather than excludes people from political and economic life, so it helps to nurture the democratic process; as it gives people the confidence and the means to reduce family size, so it helps to slow population growth; and as it gives the poor a stake in the future, so it helps to safeguard the environment.

For almost half a century, the world has been distracted from these great tasks by military conflict and ideological division. War, and the threat of war, have diverted our physical and financial resources, our science and technology, our ingenuity and imagination, and our human capacity and concern. That threat is receding. The time has therefore come for the world to recommit itself to the task of ending the age-old evils of absolute poverty, malnutrition, illiteracy, and preventable disease and to build again towards a new world order which will reflect mankind's brightest hopes rather than its darkest fears.

The ten propositions:

1   *That the promise of the World Summit for Children should be kept and that a new world order should bring an end to malnutrition, preventable disease, and illiteracy among so many millions of the world's children.*

2   *That the principle of 'first call for children' - meaning that protection for the growing bodies and minds of the young ought to have a first call on societies' resources - should become an accepted ethic of a new world order.*

3   *That if the issues of malnutrition, preventable disease, and widespread illiteracy, are not confronted as a new world order evolves, then it will be very much more difficult to reduce the rate of population growth and make the transition to environmentally sustainable development.*

4   *That the growing consensus around the importance of market economic policies should be accompanied by a corresponding consensus on the responsibility of governments to guarantee basic investments in people.*

5   *That increases in international aid should be based on a sustained and measurable commitment to meeting minimum human needs and for maintaining, in difficult times, the principle of a first call for children.*

6   *That international action on debt, aid, and trade should create an environment in which economic reform in the developing world can succeed in allowing its people to earn a decent living.*

7   *That a process of demilitarization should begin in the developing world and that, in step with that process, falling military expenditures in the industrialized nations should be linked to significant increases in international aid for development and for the resolution of common global problems.*

8   *That the chains of Africa's debt be struck off and that the continent be given sufficient external support to allow internal reform to succeed in regenerating the momentum of development.*

9   *That a new world order should oppose the apartheid of gender as vigorously as the apartheid of race.*

10   *That the responsible planning of births is one of the most effective and least expensive ways of improving the quality of life on earth - both now and in the future - and that one of the greatest mistakes of our times is the failure to realise that potential.*

Keeping the promise

Proposition: *That the promise of the World Summit for Children should be kept and that a new world order should bring an end to malnutrition, preventable disease, and illiteracy among so many millions of the world's children.*

A quarter of a million of the world's young children are dying every week,[1] and millions more are surviving in the half-life of malnutrition and almost permanent ill health.

This is not a threatened tragedy or an impending crisis. It happened today. It will happen again tomorrow. And by any objective standard of scale or severity, this issue would rank in importance with any on the human agenda. But in practice, such problems have had little purchase on priority because they are primarily the problems of the poor and the powerless.

The children who are the victims of preventable malnutrition, disease, and illiteracy are being most shamefully failed by the present world order. But in the last two years, that failure has begun to feature on the political agenda in a way that is unprecedented in UNICEF's 40-year history.

The most important signal of that new priority was the convening of the *World Summit for Children* on 29 and 30 September, 1990. Over those two days, the largest ever gathering of heads of state met to consider the possibility of bringing to an end, in our times, the long-running tragedy described in the opening paragraphs of this chapter.

Closing the gap

The *Summit* met at a point when it was becoming clear that one of the greatest humanitarian goals of this century - immunizing 80% of the world's children against six major diseases by the end of 1990 - was going to be met (panel 3). That achievement is now saving the lives of over 3 million children each year.[2] It has also demonstrated, after a decade-long effort, that the world now has the outreach capacity to bridge the gap between mass-scale problems and inexpensive solutions.

Influenced by that example, the *Summit* concluded with a commitment,[3] now signed by more than one hundred and twenty heads of state, to begin applying today's accumulated knowledge and inexpensive techniques to a range of basic problems facing the world's children (panel 1).

The immunization achievement had also shown the usefulness of having a quantifiable target as a focus for national efforts and international support. The *Summit* therefore formulated its commitments as a range of specific goals which all nations would strive to achieve by the end of this century. Those basic goals, set out in full on page 61, include: a reduction of child death rates by at least one third (fig. 1); a halving of maternal mortality rates; a halving of severe and moderate malnutrition among the under-fives (fig. 2); 90% immunization coverage (panel 13); a 95% fall in deaths from measles; an end to polio and tetanus; clean water and safe sanitation for all families; a basic education for all children and completion of primary school for at least 80%; the availability, to all couples, of family planning services; and observance by all nations of the *Convention on the Rights of the Child*.

These goals were arrived at by a process of consultation between governments and

The year 2000 goals: one for all and all for one

1

For the 1990s, there is a broad agreement that progress is best achieved if market forces do what market forces do best and governments do what governments do best. In particular, it is government that must guarantee the long-term investment in people, in their health, nutrition and education, without which economic progress will be both slowed in pace and deprived of purpose.

In September 1990 the World Summit for Children, bringing together leaders from over 150 nations including 71 Presidents and Prime Ministers, translated the idea of 'investing in people' into a set of specific goals for the year 2000. The Summit Declaration also promised a new political commitment, long the missing link between what can be done and what will be done. Programmes of action for reaching the year 2000 goals will be drawn up by most nations before the end of 1991 (panel 2).

The goals, twenty-seven in all,[1] include a one-third reduction in child deaths, a halving of child malnutrition, a halving of deaths among women during pregnancy and childbirth, universally available family planning, safe water and sanitation for all, and basic education for all children. More specific child health goals include 90% immunization, polio eradication, the elimination of neonatal tetanus, a 95% reduction in measles deaths (currently about 840,000 each year), a halving of child deaths caused by diarrhoea (4 million a year), and a one-third reduction in child deaths from pneumonia (3 million a year).

At first sight, taking on so many targets seems over ambitious. But the 'one for all, all for one' relationship between them makes it feasible. Reducing child malnutrition, for example, sharply reduces child deaths. Reduced child deaths means that more parents become interested in family planning. More family planning improves maternal and child health, leading in turn to better nutrition and fewer deaths. The more that is known about such synergisms, the stronger the case for tackling all of the year 2000 goals either together or in close sequence.

In setting the new goals, the *Summit for Children* was encouraged by success in reaching an earlier global target - 80% child immunization - which had been set in the late 1970s at a time when vaccination coverage was running at little more than 10%. It is a success that offers more than moral encouragement. Immunizing 80% has meant building a system that can deliver vaccines to 100 million infants four or five times a year. The organizational legacy of all this, if sustained and strengthened in the 1990s, could help achieve many of the new goals. And as with immunization, a variety of low-cost techniques are now available for preventing or treating the problems that cause at least three quarters of all today's child deaths and child malnutrition.

At the *Summit for Children*, the world's leaders also agreed "*to make available the resources to meet these commitments*". The total cost has been estimated at $20 billion a year throughout the 1990s and at least one third of this would need to come from increases in, or a reallocation of, international aid.

This extra aid required amounts to less than 1% of the industrialized world's current military expenditures - surely not too high a price, in the post cold war era, to save the lives of many millions of children, prevent the malnutrition of many millions more, slow the world's rate of population growth, and make the greatest of all investments in the future.

Fig. 1 Child deaths

The *World Summit for Children* has set the target of a one third reduction in under-five deaths by the year 2000 (or a reduction to 70 per 1000 births – whichever is lower).

The chart shows the progress in reducing child deaths from 1960 to 1990. The white lines indicate the progress each region will have to achieve if the year 2000 target is to be met.

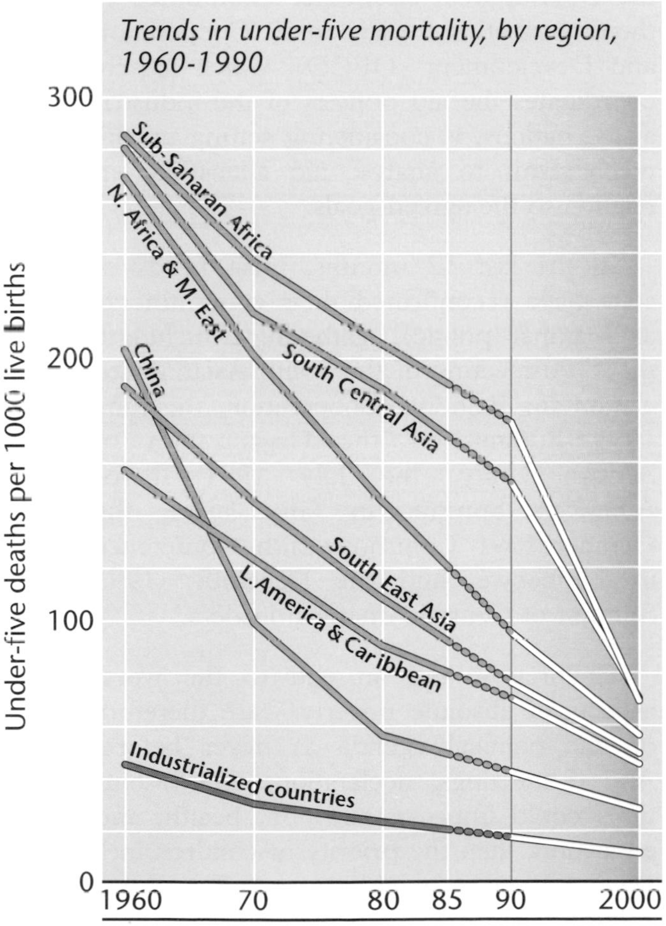

Trends in under-five mortality, by region, 1960-1990

Under-five deaths per 1000 live births

Sub-Saharan Africa
N. Africa & M. East
China
South Central Asia
South East Asia
L. America & Caribbean
Industrialized countries

300
200
100
0

1960   70   80   85   90   2000

The chart does not accurately reflect changes in under-five death rates in the second half of the 1980s as recent figures are not available for many countries. In particular, the doubling of immunization coverage since 1985 has significantly reduced deaths. But in some countries, the decline has been slowed by the debt crisis and adjustment to recession during this same period.

Source: UNICEF estimates based primarily on data from the UN Population Division which include South Africa as part of the Sub-Saharan Africa region.

the specialized agencies of the United Nations. They are based on a review of the specific, low-cost opportunities now available. They therefore represent a comprehensive programme for narrowing the gap that has been allowed to open between the availability of low-cost technologies and their application to those in need.

The agreement to that programme, by virtually every nation, marks the rejection of the long-held notion that the problem of malnutrition and disease is so vast and inevitable that nothing significant can be done. In its place has come the recognition that the great majority of child deaths, and of the vast weight of illness and malnutrition which lie behind them, can now be prevented relatively cheaply and easily.

From promise to practice

One of the first consequences of the *Summit* has been to accelerate the progress of the *Convention on the Rights of the Child*.[4] The *Convention* seeks to establish minimum standards for children's survival, health and nutrition and minimum standards of protection against all forms of exploitation and abuse. In the two years since the text was adopted by the General Assembly of the United Nations, it has been ratified by over 100 nations - a process which commonly requires a decade or more. The *Convention* therefore takes its place alongside the commitments made at the *World Summit for Children* as a sign of a new political priority for children and of a new promise of protection in the decade ahead.

It is too early to tell to what extent the declarations of the *Summit* and the signing of the *Convention* represent rhetoric which will echo ever more faintly down the years ahead. In some nations, it is already becoming clear that they represent a solid intent which is already being translated into practical action (panel 2).

One of the first tests will be the drawing up of the detailed *national* programmes of action for achieving the *Summit* goals. All countries represented at the *Summit* agreed to formulate such programmes by the end of 1991. By October 1991, 60 countries had reached this first stage and that number is expected to surpass 100 early in 1992. Some middle-income developing countries such as Peru and Mexico have begun implementing their programmes knowing that most of the funds will have to come through the difficult process of re-allocating internal resources. Other programmes, especially those being drawn up by the countries of sub-Saharan Africa, will have little chance of being put into practice unless at least 50% of the cost is met by increased aid. In total, it is estimated that the financial resources required to reach all of the year 2000 goals amount to an additional $20 billion a year.[5] Of that sum, two thirds might be found by the developing countries themselves and one third might be made available in additional aid (though the proportions will vary from region to region). The $20 billion total is about the same as the world now spends on the military *every week*.[6]

As agreed at the *Summit*, many industrialized nations have been reviewing the situation of children in their own countries and examining their aid programmes to see how they might better serve the *Summit* goals. The recent decision by the Netherlands to grant $7.5 million for debt relief for children's programmes in Ecuador, Honduras, and Jamaica (which will buy back debt of at least twice that amount in local currencies) is one of the first tangible results. To monitor the process, the Development Assistance Committee of the Organization for Economic Cooperation and Development (OECD), which loosely coordinates the aid policies of the industrialized nations, is considering setting up the mechanisms to analyse aid allocations in relation to the agreed goals.

In the last 12 months, most heads of state have reconfirmed their commitments at regional political gatherings, including the 1990 meeting of the South Asian Association for Regional Cooperation, the June 1991 Summit of the Organization of African Unity, the July 1991 Ibero-American Summit in Guadalajara, the October 1991 Commonwealth Conference in Zimbabwe, and the December 1991 Summit of Central American leaders.

Children - and an end to the worst aspects of absolute poverty - are therefore on the political agenda as never before. And if meetings, declarations and resolutions could improve nutrition, health, and education, then the priority of children in a new world order would be assured.

These unprecedented political commitments represent an opportunity not to be missed. It has long been lamented that what was lacking was not the means or even the resources but the political will to tackle these great problems. The events of the last two years represent the greatest promise

Fig. 2 Progress against malnutrition

The 1990 *World Summit for Children* set the goal of halving child malnutrition by the year 2000. As the chart shows, this will require an acceleration of past progress. Almost no comparative data exist for Africa.

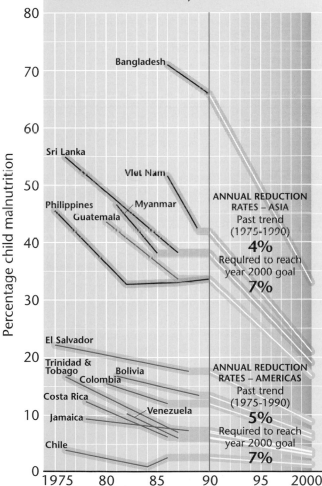

Halving child malnutrition: past trends and future requirements, selected countries, Asia and the Americas, 1975-2000

ANNUAL REDUCTION RATES – ASIA
Past trend
(1975-1990)
4%
Required to reach year 2000 goal
7%

ANNUAL REDUCTION RATES – AMERICAS
Past trend
(1975-1990)
5%
Required to reach year 2000 goal
7%

The level of malnutrition for 1990 is set by the most recent estimate available for each country.
Malnutrition is defined as more than two standard deviations below the desirable weight for age, and child malnutrition refers to the child population under the age of five.

Source: UNICEF estimates 1991.

that has ever been made to the world's children, and the greatest opportunity for building sustained political support for their cause. It is now time for all concerned individuals and organizations in all countries to mobilize behind that commitment.

Participation

The *World Summit for Children* and the *Convention on the Rights of the Child* are part of a process that has already yielded extraordinary practical results in the last few years. The key to that process has been political commitment from national leaderships followed by the mobilization of a wide range of resources to see that commitment through. The immunization achievement, for example, began in the 1980s with declarations and public commitments by political leaders; it has since been translated into action with the support of many hundreds of thousands of people in both developing and industrialized worlds.

By the mid-1980s, most heads of state in the developing world had made and signed political commitments to the 80% immunization goal (fig. 3). The sheer scale of the professional and public mobilization that followed is sometimes difficult to grasp from the perspective of the industrialized world. From lowly beginnings in the late 1970s and early 1980s, a system has been built which now reaches over 100 million infants - and their parents - on five separate occasions each year. Against all logistical difficulties, this means that over 500 million separate contacts are now being made each year between modern health services and children.[7] The result of this effort - the

Mexico: keeping the promise

2

Most countries are now preparing National Programmes of Action (NPAs) for reaching the goals agreed at the 1990 *World Summit for Children*. By October 1991, 60 countries had finalized their plans and that number is expected to reach almost 100 by the end of the year. The targets include a one-third reduction in child deaths, a halving of child malnutrition, and primary school education for at least 80% (page 61).

Many countries are already beginning to translate the promise into practice. One example is Mexico, whose President, Carlos Salinas de Gortari, was one of the six initiators of the *Summit*.

Towards the end of 1990, President Salinas called a meeting of senior ministers to decide how Mexico would go about achieving the *Summit* goals. It was to be the first in a series of six-monthly cabinet reviews - chaired by the President - to monitor progress for the nation's children. To coordinate planning, the Ministers of Health and Education and other senior government officials were appointed to a National Commission for the Achievement of the Summit Goals.

By November 1991, Mexico's own NPA, complete with baseline data for 1990, specific Mexican targets for 1994 and 2000, and recommendations for a system to monitor progress - was approved by the government.

Meanwhile, UNICEF was also being approached by the Mayor of Mexico City (population 18 million), plus other mayors and state governors, for assistance in a renewed national effort for children.

In all countries, some restructuring of government budgets will be necessary if the year 2000 goals are to be achieved. One of the first practical actions in Mexico has been a 40% increase in the budget of PRONASOL, the government programme which aims to provide basic services to the poorest fifth of Mexico's people and which is to be a main vehicle for moving the country towards the year 2000 goals. PRONASOL will now receive $1.7 billion in 1991 - over 8% of the government's total social expenditure.

Other actions for children in 1991 include:

○ Basic health services provided through PRONASOL have been made available to 15 million people in the poorest villages and city neighbourhoods - a 25% increase over 1990.

○ Seven out of 31 states, plus Mexico City, have pushed immunization coverage to 90% of under-fives. Mexico's NPA aims at almost 100% coverage by October 1992.

○ Distribution of ORS - to protect children against dehydration caused by diarrhoea - has risen to 20 million packets per year.

○ A Mexican version of *Facts for Life* has been produced (panel 16) with 380,000 copies published to date and 1 million planned by end of 1994.

○ The WHO/UNICEF code - *Ten steps to successful breastfeeding* - is being made standard practice in one hospital in each state and four in Mexico City (panel 12). These 35 hospitals have 'baby-friendly hospital' status and will act as models for all maternity units in the country.

○ Three million more people were provided with drinking water in 1991, bringing the total served to 70% of Mexico's population. The aim is 84% by 1994 and 100% by 2000.

As in all other countries, it remains to be seen whether Mexico's commitment to achieving the *Summit* goals can be sustained in the face of all the difficulties which lie ahead in the 1990s. But in the first year after the *World Summit for Children*, it is clear that protecting the lives and the normal development of the nation's children has assumed a new political priority.

Fig. 3 The immunization achievement

In the late 1970s, when immunization reached only about 10 percent of the developing world's children, the international community set the ambitious target of 80 percent immunization by the end of 1990. The chart shows the results of the ten-year effort.

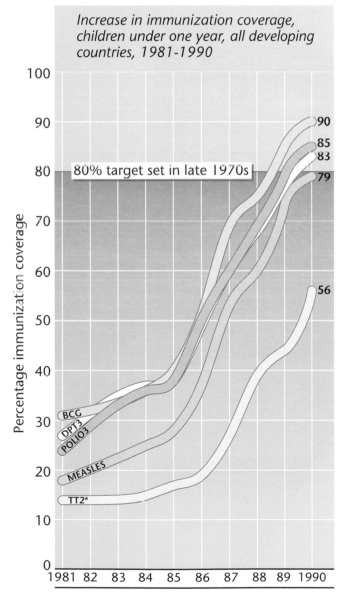

Increase in immunization coverage, children under one year, all developing countries, 1981-1990

Percentage immunization coverage

80% target set in late 1970s

BCG
DPT3
POLIO3
MEASLES
TT2*

90
85
83
79
56

1981 82 83 84 85 86 87 88 89 1990

The years 1981 to 1985 exclude figures for China
* For pregnant women

Source: WHO and UNICEF, August 1991.

largest international operation ever mounted in peacetime - is that *the lives of almost 9,000 children are being saved every day* (fig. 4). Another result is that there are today almost 2 million children who are walking, running and playing normally in the developing world who would have been crippled by polio were it not for the immunization efforts of the last ten years. And as child malnutrition is caused more by the frequency of infection than by the lack of food,[8] the prevention of disease on this scale has also helped to protect the normal growth of even larger numbers of the world's children. For the future, the immunization effort has laid the foundations of an outreach system which can now begin to make available other key elements of primary health care as well as delivering new vaccines as and when they become available (panels 14 and 15).

Also in the early and mid-1980s, more than 50 of the developing world's heads of state made a commitment to making widely available a method of preventing dehydration known as oral rehydration therapy (ORT). This simple and almost costless technique can enable parents themselves to prevent or treat the dehydration induced by diarrhoeal disease. At the time, ORT was little known outside scientific circles. Today, the participation of millions of people has carried this life-saving knowledge to at least one third of all the families in the developing world (fig. 5). The result is the saving of over 1 million children's lives each year.[9]

The practical importance of this achievement, too, can easily be overlooked from the balconies of affluence. Dehydration induced by diarrhoeal disease has killed an estimated 150 million young children in the forty years of UNICEF's existence - more than the combined civilian and military deaths of both world wars. It remains one of the biggest killers of children in the modern world. A simple and inexpensive method of treating or preventing that dehydration has been available for 20 years. In scale, it is as if a cure for cancer had been discovered and then not used. But today, the long-overdue move to put the knowledge and the means of preventing the deaths and the malnutrition caused by diarrhoeal disease has now begun in earnest.

Such achievements demonstrate the potential of political commitments combined with the dedication of the professional services and the participation of large numbers of people. The expertise and the leadership of the health services has obviously been indispensable, but the health services alone could not have brought about achievements on this scale. Reaching out to many hundreds of millions of families with information about ORT, or information about the when and the where and the why of immunization, has been achieved with the participation of the schools and the mass media, the churches, mosques and temples, the political parties and professional bodies, the business community and the trades unions, the non-governmental and voluntary organizations, the women's groups and the people's movements.

Many governments in the industrialized world have given financial and technical support (not least through UNICEF which is the largest international supplier of the vaccines used in reaching the immunization goal) and many non-governmental organizations in both industrialized and

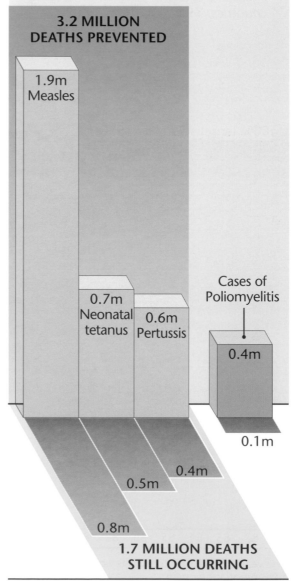

Fig. 4 Three million saved

The achievement of the 80 percent immunization target in the developing world is now preventing over three million child deaths each year.

Deaths prevented and still occurring, from vaccine preventable diseases, in millions, all developing countries, 1991

3.2 MILLION DEATHS PREVENTED

1.9m Measles

0.7m Neonatal tetanus

0.6m Pertussis

Cases of Poliomyelitis

0.4m

0.1m

0.4m

0.5m

0.8m

1.7 MILLION DEATHS STILL OCCURRING

Source: WHO and UNICEF, August 1991.

developing nations have mobilized support from a wide public. To cite the most spectacular example, Rotary International has mobilized hundreds of thousands of its members in almost all countries, including its chapters in Africa, Asia, and Latin America, to provide volunteers and raise well over $200 million in support of vaccination against polio - the largest fund-raising effort ever undertaken by a voluntary service organization in support of a specific cause.[10]

Mobilization on a similar scale will be needed, in all countries, if the commitments made by the *World Summit for Children* are also to be converted into achievements.

The process of which the *Summit* is part, and the social changes it has already brought about, is therefore another dimension of the communications revolution and the increasing participation of people which is at the centre of contemporary political and economic change.

People's promise

The increase in both political commitment and social mobilization for children in recent years offers reasonable hope that the needs and the rights of the world's children, and particularly of those hundreds of millions who lack even the basics of health, nutrition, and education, will find a place on the agenda of the new world order that is now emerging.

On behalf of peoples as well as of governments, the *World Summit for Children* was a promise to the children of the 1990s. It was a promise to use today's knowledge, technology, resources, and communications capacity to protect their lives, their growth, their health, and their rights. It was a promise to end the quiet catastrophe of malnutrition and disease and illiteracy. And it was a promise to keep their needs and the rights on the international agenda as a new world order evolves in the decade ahead.

That promise must now be kept.

Immunization: still a bargain

3

The lives of 3.2 million children a year[2] are now being saved by the immunization efforts of the 1980s.3 In addition, there are almost 2 million children who are now walking, running and playing normally in the developing world who would have been crippled by polio were it not for the achievement of the 80% immunization goal.

But if immunization was the greatest public health success story of the 1980s, it remains the greatest public health challenge of the 1990s. By building on what has been achieved, it is possible to prevent a further 2 million child deaths each year, and to reduce the impact of vaccine-preventable disease on child malnutrition and disability.

Not only the developing world stands to gain. Polio eradication, for example, would save the United States over $114 million a year in vaccines alone.[4] The cost of eradication? Approximately $100 million a year for 10 years.[5]

The first challenge is to raise immunization levels where coverage still lags. In eastern and southern Africa, immunization reaches only 60%.[6] The aim in the 1990s must be to disaggregate the figures so that the year 2000 target of 90% is achieved in every province and, where possible, in every district.

The second challenge is to begin monitoring not just immunization levels but the decline of disease. The goals set by the *World Summit for Children* are: elimination of neonatal tetanus (536,000 deaths a year), eradication of polio (116,000 cases a year), and a 95% reduction in measles deaths (840,000 a year).

Third, there is the challenge of adding vaccines such as hepatitis B (panel 15) to the immunization system and stepping up research on the children's vaccine initiative (panel 14).

But by far the greatest challenge of the decade will be to begin building on the organizational achievement of 80% immunization in order to provide more comprehensive primary health care.

The institutional legacy of immunization is a system that now makes more than 500 million separate contacts between health services and children every year.[7] That system is now beginning to be used to deliver other vital elements of primary health care such as vitamin A and iodine supplements.[8] Much more remains to be done. And the more the system is used, the lower the unit cost of each service it delivers and the more sustainable it becomes.

Even more fundamentally, the immunization effort has made a breakthrough towards primary health care by mobilizing social resources and communications channels behind a major health improvement. It has therefore helped make health into a social and not just a medical responsibility.

For many of the health services involved, reaching for the immunization goal has meant reaching also for a new idea of who the real customers are - not the people who walk through clinic doors but the entire population of a given area. Going out into the community to record every single infant in need of vaccination has begun the process of ordered and regular contact between health services and every family.

"*The effort has not only strengthened existing primary health care systems*", says a UNICEF senior adviser on the immunization effort in the 1980s, "*it has also mobilized a far wider section of society towards a recognized social goal. A new level of responsibility has been developed between health services and the community served ... a new level of expectation and commitment to serve. These, in the long run, are the greatest benefits of the immunization effort, and the factors most likely to account for its sustainability and eventual expansion to a truly universal programme providing far more than immunization services to each and every child.*"[9]

First call for children

Proposition: *That the principle of 'first call for children' - meaning that protection for the growing bodies and minds of the young ought to have a first call on societies' resources - should become an accepted ethic of a new world order.*

The *World Summit for Children* called upon all nations to be guided by the principle of a 'first call for children' - *"a principle that the essential needs of all children should be given high priority in the allocation of resources, in bad times as well as in good times, at national and international levels as well as at family levels."*[11]

The principle of first call for children is founded not only on the sands of sentiment. Most of the mental and physical development of the human being occurs in the first few years of life. Those years are the child's one and only chance to develop normally in brain and body and to grow to his or her genetic potential. If the various stages of that development are not completed at the appropriate time, then lasting damage may be done to the complex processes of growth. There is no second chance. It is on the bedrock of this physiological fact that the principle of first call is built. And it is therefore a principle which demands that, even in the worst of times, the protection afforded to children should be the last element of social protection to be relinquished rather than the first to be sacrificed.

The principle of first call is practised by many parents in all countries. But the process of advancing civilization is essentially a process of institutionalising these finer feelings and higher principles which human beings intermittently show themselves capable of. And it is in institutionalising the ethic of first call, in automatically embodying that principle in the conduct of its affairs, that mankind has so far failed to take the step forward for civilization which such a change would represent.

Because the child has only one opportunity for growth, and because the process of that growth is so subtle and susceptible, the essence of the principle of first call is that protection should be not just a priority but an absolute. In other words, the child should be able to depend on that commitment at all times and through all difficulties, rather than being at the mercy of shifting circumstance and competing priorities.

In particular, the very essentials of child development - love and caring attention, normal physical growth, immunization against disease, basic health care, and the opportunity to go to school - should be a commitment which all societies make and maintain in good times and in bad. That commitment should not waver in times of economic recession; it should not give way to the short-term demands of structural adjustment programmes; it should not bow to the pressures of particular interest groups; it should not fluctuate with the fortunes of particular political parties; it should not be shaken in times of turbulence or transition; it should not be subordinated to any ideology; it should not even be suspended in times of war or civil strife. It is in such times of stress that the principle of first call should be most tenaciously adhered to but is in practice most frequently relinquished.

From UNICEF's perspective, it is the events of the last decade which demand that this principle of first call be vigorously advanced as a new world order begins to take shape. In crisis after crisis, and in country after country, this organization has witnessed the consequences of that principle not being in place. Whether the cause be the debt crisis and structural adjustment in Africa and Latin America, or the turbulence of political and economic transition in Central and Eastern Europe, or the shift in the political philosophies of many industrialized countries (panel 5), or the outbreak of wars in Africa[12] or in the Gulf, it is children whose lives are the most devastated, children who will bear the scars for longest, and children who are paying the ultimate price with the loss of their one opportunity to grow normally, to be educated, and to acquire the skills necessary to earn a living for themselves and their families in the 21st century.

So little heed is paid to the consequence for children of the mistakes and excesses of the adult world that there are virtually no mechanisms for sensitively monitoring their nutritional status, their patterns of disease, or their levels of enrolment in school. Even in times of turbulence and transition, when all experience says that children will be most at risk, it is still easier to ascertain how many video recorders have been imported or sold in any given month than it is to find out what has happened to the health and nutrition of a nation's children.

We do know that it is children who have paid the heaviest price for the developing world's debts. Fragmentary evidence, pieced together by UNICEF over the last decade,[13] has shown a picture of rising malnutrition, and in some cases rising child deaths, in some of the most heavily indebted

countries of Africa and Latin America.[14] Surveys by UNESCO[15] have also shown that the attempt to adjust economies to the debt crisis has caused school enrolment ratios among 6 to 11 year-olds to fall in at least 50 of the most debt-ridden nations of the developing world.

We also know, to take another example, that it is young children who are at this moment paying the heaviest price for the Gulf war. In the first study of its kind ever undertaken, it has been found that child mortality rates have increased steeply in Iraq over the last year.[16] Without widespread acceptance of the principle of first call, modern warfare will continue to be a war against children (panel 6).

Similarly, it is children who are bearing the brunt of the hardships being endured by Central and Eastern Europe as old economic systems finally collapse under the weight of their own inadequacies and nation after nation makes its brave transition (panel 4). A special study by UNICEF's International Child Development Centre in Florence,[17] published earlier this year, has shown that health and education services have been subject to some of the deepest spending cuts and that the nutritional status of many children may already be threatened. In Albania - the worst case - approximately 20% of all children are now malnourished and infant mortality has doubled from its 1989 level.[18]

As described in panel 5, children have also suffered most in the less dramatic transitions in political and economic philosophy which have occurred in many of the industrialized nations over the last decade.[19] In the United States, for example, the proportion of

Fig. 5 One third use ORT

ORT is an inexpensive method by which families themselves can prevent and treat dehydration – which kills more than two million young children each year. The technique has been taught to one third of the developing world's families in the 1980s and is now preventing over one million child deaths each year.

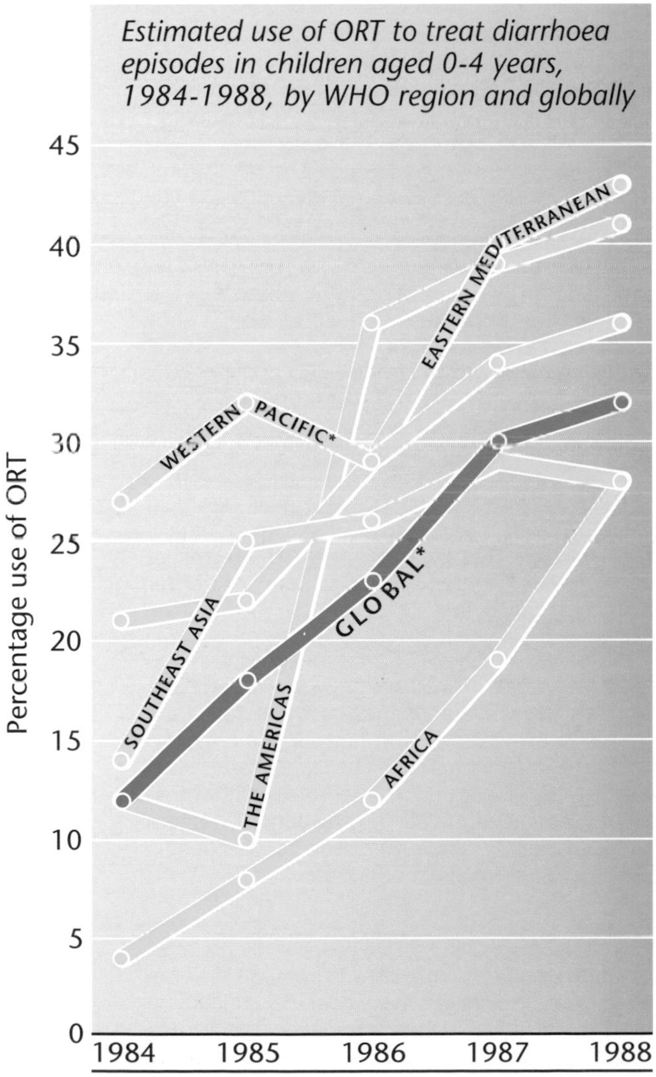

Estimated use of ORT to treat diarrhoea episodes in children aged 0-4 years, 1984-1988, by WHO region and globally

* Excluding China

ORT includes specially formulated oral rehydration salts, sugar salt solutions, and recommended home fluids.

Source: World Health Organization, Geneva, 1990.

children living in poverty has risen from 14% in the 1960s to approximately 22% today.[20]

In the past, it may have been in some degree inevitable that the well-being of children should be subject to the vicissitudes of the adult world. But today the very basics of child protection, which are at the same time the very basics of protection for society's future, need not be so readily relinquished. With today's new capacities, low-cost protection for the health, nutrition, and education of almost all children is possible in almost all circumstances. By national action where possible, and with international support where not, conscious and specific policies can be put in place to protect the basic needs and rights of children even in the worst of times.

A new world order, if it is to represent progress for civilization, must therefore absorb into itself the principle that the shocks and the set-backs, the mistakes and the mismanagements which will always play some part in human affairs, must never again be translated into rising malnutrition, disease, death, and illiteracy among the most vulnerable members of society.

Some nations have shown, in recent years, that it is possible to begin putting this principle into practice. The Republic of Korea has ensured, in each of the temporary economic reversals of the 1970s and 1980s, that specific policies were in place to prevent rising oil prices or falling agricultural output from being translated into worsening levels of health, nutrition, or education among its children. The government of Indonesia, under economic pressure from the slump in oil prices in the

Eastern Europe: transition with a human face

4

'First call for children' is especially important in times of crisis. Whether in economic recession, political upheaval, or armed conflict, specific policies are needed to protect the child's one opportunity to grow normally in mind and body.

UNICEF has advocated this principle for the developing countries as they adopt adjustment policies to cope with debt and recession. But a new UNICEF study,[10] published in 1991, shows that the principle is also relevant to economic turbulence in Central and Eastern Europe.

The two processes have much in common. In both, 'adjustment' has involved spending cuts and the withdrawal of subsidies on food and other essentials. And in both, the capacity of families to meet their needs by their own efforts has been undermined by unemployment, falling incomes, and rising prices. At the same time, cuts in social services have weakened the 'safety nets' just when the strain on them was increasing.

Unemployment in Hungary increased tenfold between late 1989 and May 1991. In Poland, the end of 1991 unemployment figure is expected to be 2 million - almost 15% of the labour force. Czechoslovakia expects half a million unemployed by the end of 1992. For those in work, incomes have fallen steeply. Average real incomes in Poland fell by 25% in the first nine months of 1990. In Bulgaria, the fall has been nearer 50%. In Czechoslovakia, the number of officially poor is expected to quadruple in 1991. In Poland and the USSR, 40% now live below the official poverty line.

Cutting subsidies has changed relative prices and many families are now spending 50% to 60% of income on food alone. The consumption of bread, milk, and other basic foods is known to have declined in Bulgaria, Hungary, Poland, the USSR and Yugoslavia. In Albania - the worst case - approximately 20% of all children are now malnourished, and infant mortality is more than double its 1989 level of 15 per 1,000 births.[11]

'Social income' has also declined. Minimum wages, unemployment benefits, child allowances, old-age pensions, and disability pay, have been theoretically maintained, but in practice they have been pared away by inflation. Companies have also abandoned welfare services formerly provided to employees' families. Czechoslovakia cut spending on health by 20% in 1990 and on education by 10% in each of the last two years.

In part, the inadequacy of social safety nets is a result of miscalculations about the weight they would have to bear. Poland, for example, planned for unemployment rising to 400,000 and incomes falling by 5% to 10%: in the event, unemployment rose to 1.4 million by December 1990 and average incomes fell by 27%.

The worst human consequences of all this could almost certainly have been avoided. Unfortunately, there are signs that the baby of minimum welfare measures is being thrown out with the bath water of state control.

Reasonable indexing of benefits, sensitive monitoring of changes in child well-being, careful targeting of available resources, free school meals, food stamps to ensure minimum nutritional standards, and the maintenance of basic health and education services - all of these could have protected the most vulnerable, and especially the children, as Eastern Europe makes its brave transition to democratic politics and free-market economies.

As in the developing world, the rich nations could play a specific role by helping to maintain minimum standards of health and nutrition at a time when governments are having acute difficulty in doing so. In other words, international aid could help to uphold the principle of 'first call' by making sure that children do not suffer most in times of turbulence and transition. And in doing so, it would also help to ensure that long-term progress is not undermined by short-term exigencies.

early 1980s, took a conscious decision to cut back spending on industrial projects and on hospital building in order to maintain expenditures on rural health clinics, immunization programmes, and primary schools.[21] In the 1980s, Chile[22] and Costa Rica[23] succeeded in maintaining the downward trend in infant mortality by establishing specific nutrition and health programmes to protect the poorest children from the harsh economic ride of that decade. Also in the 1980s, Botswana has managed to shield its children from the worst effects of severe drought by setting up sensitive monitoring systems in order to target government support, including food subsidies. Zimbabwe, also, managed to prevent any increase in child malnutrition during the droughts and recessions of the 1980s and it has done so by means of specific low-cost policies which have included primary health care programmes, immunization services, diarrhoeal disease control measures, supplementary feeding programmes, and rural water supplies.

There is also some evidence to suggest that the principle of first call may be beginning to establish itself even in times of war and civil strife. El Salvador has not allowed its long and bitter civil war to waive the rights of its children to the benefits of immunization; on three separate 'days of tranquility' each year for the last seven years that war has been suspended so that almost all the nation's children could be vaccinated. More recently, the idea of 'corridors of tranquility', through which essential supplies can reach civilian families and their children, has been accepted in Sudan (the Nile is also now open as a route for relief supplies). In Ethiopia, two similar corridors of peace were kept open until the end of the war earlier this year. In Angola, six such corridors were opened in 1991. In Iraq, UNICEF and WHO were able to open a channel for shipping the most essential health supplies even at the height of the Gulf conflict.

Such examples strike the sparks of hope for a principle which must become a steady flame in the years ahead. In every set-back and crisis, in every period of transition or turbulence, whether caused by natural disaster, civil war, international conflict, economic mismanagement, or political change, it should be axiomatic, nationally and internationally, to ask what the effect on children is likely to be and what specific policies are needed to shield their growing minds and bodies from the sharpest edges of change.

In the attempt to kindle that flame, the world now has the advantage of a virtually universal agreement on the minimum protection which should be guaranteed to children. In the goals of the *World Summit for Children* and the provisions of the *Convention on the Rights of the Child*, are set out the agreed minimum standards for the protection of children's survival, health, and education and the agreed minimum protection required by all children, in all nations, against exploitation and abuse whether in war, at work, or in the home.

The world therefore now has a set of agreed criteria against which any and all nations can measure practical progress towards a new order for children.

Fig. 6 Child deaths and child births

Each line on the chart represents, for one developing country, the change in under-five mortality rate (U5MR) and total fertility rate (TFR) over the period from 1960 to 1989. The intermediate point on each line represents the point at 1980.

Almost all developing countries are represented on the chart. It shows that the initial steep falls in under-five death rates were often not accompanied by any significant change in fertility. Later, when under-five deaths fall still further, the pattern becomes mixed – with some countries showing significant falls in fertility and some not. In the later stages, further reduction of under-five deaths is – with very few exceptions – accompanied by even steeper falls in births.

On the right hand side of the graph is shown the present under-five mortality rate of some of the most populous developing countries today. It can be seen that most are close to the level at which further falls in under-five deaths could be expected to be accompanied by even steeper falls in births.

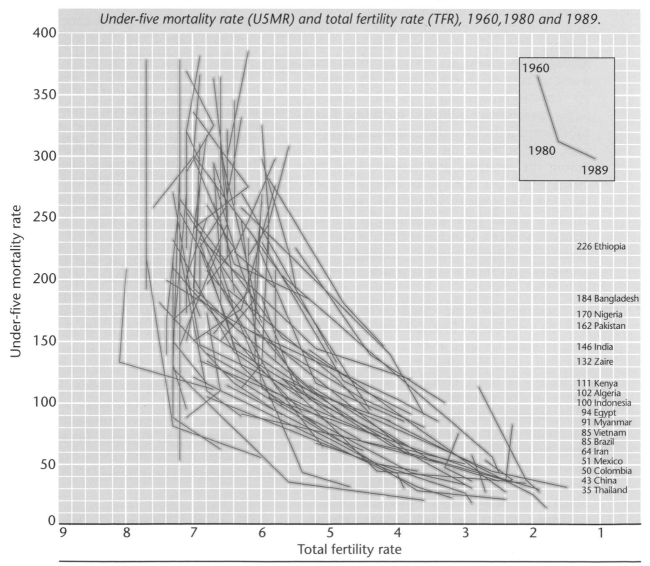

Under-five mortality rate (U5MR) and total fertility rate (TFR), 1960, 1980 and 1989.

226 Ethiopia

184 Bangladesh
170 Nigeria
162 Pakistan

146 India
132 Zaire

111 Kenya
102 Algeria
100 Indonesia
94 Egypt
91 Myanmar
85 Vietnam
85 Brazil
64 Iran
51 Mexico
50 Colombia
43 China
35 Thailand

Under-five mortality rate

Total fertility rate

Source: UNICEF, adapted from data supplied by the United Nations Population Division.

Fewer deaths, fewer births

Proposition: *That if the issues of malnutrition, preventable disease, and widespread illiteracy, are not confronted as a new world order evolves, then it will be very much more difficult to reduce the rate of population growth and make the transition to environmentally sustainable development.*

Public support for the cause of protecting children against malnutrition and disease has sometimes been inhibited by the argument that, inasmuch as such efforts were successful, they would ultimately be self-defeating because they would serve only to exacerbate the problem of rapid population growth.

This argument is morally and demographically unsound. As last year's *State of the World's Children* showed in some detail, reducing child deaths is one of the most powerful of the forces which make up the reins of population growth.

Four factors are most strongly associated with falling birth rates. Those four horsemen of the non-apocalypse are: rising incomes, female education, reduced child deaths, and the availability of family planning. When pulling together, they exert many times more control on birth rates than any one of them acting alone. There is therefore no conflict between meeting the needs of people and controlling the growth of population; indeed all of the propositions advanced in this report would contribute in some way towards a more rapid slowing-down in the rate of population growth.

The particular link between reduced child deaths and reduced births is one of the least understood and most vital of contemporary issues. In general, lowering the rate of child deaths helps also to lower the rate of births because it increases parental confidence in the predictability of family building and reduces the need for many births as a means of insuring against, or compensating for, the possibility of child death.[24] *"It might be thought,"* says the 1991 *Human Development Report* from the United Nations Development Programme, *"that, if more children survived, population problems would get worse. Quite the reverse. Fertility tends to drop when parents are more confident that their children will survive."*

But the strength of this relationship between falling deaths and falling births depends on the particular stage which a country has reached (fig. 6). In the earlier stages, when under-five mortality rates first begin to fall from a very high level, parental confidence remains low and birth rates tend to change little. Most countries in the developing world have now completed this phase. In the next stage, when under-five mortality rates begin to fall below 200 per 1,000 live births, the correlation between falling deaths and falling births is still weak. But it is when countries begin to bring child mortality rates down below 150, as is happening now in countries such as India, and to move towards and through the 100 barrier, that strong and consistent patterns of fertility change begin to emerge. At this stage, most countries begin to see a much more rapid fall in the number of births for every further advance that is made in reducing child deaths.

This is good news which has so far gone unheard. For the great majority of coun-

The United States: the rise and rise of child poverty

5

'First call for children' should not be a problem for rich nations. But in the most prosperous nation of all, child deprivation has increased even as wealth has risen and poverty among other age groups has fallen.

In the 1960s, the proportion of US children living in poverty was halved from 27% to 14%. In the 1970s, it crept back to 17%. Then, in the 1980s, it rose again to 22%[12] - even in a decade of almost uninterrupted economic growth and a near 25% increase in America's GNP.

Over the same 30 year period, overall poverty in the United States, and especially among the elderly, has declined. Driven mainly by government action, the proportion of older citizens (65+) living in poverty fell by more than two thirds.

So why has a nation with the demonstrated capacity to reduce poverty failed to do so for its children? *Child Poverty in America,*[13] a report from the Washington-based Children's Defense Fund (CDF), clears the way for its answer by exploding some myths.

The stock image of the black child born to an unmarried, unemployed mother living on welfare in a big city is a description which fits fewer than one in ten of America's poor children. Inner-city blacks and Hispanics are certainly over-represented, but a majority of America's 12 million poor children are white. Most live outside big cities. Most live in families with only one or two children. And most belong to households where at least one parent works.

The main reasons for rising child poverty are, first, the erosion of benefits provided by government to poor families with children and, second, the steady fall in real wages among America's unskilled.

The average weekly wage of non-supervisory workers fell by approximately 20% between 1973 and 1990. At the same time, the government's commitment to a minimum 'family wage' appears to have faded; even after recent increases, the real minimum wage in 1990 is 20% less than it was in 1980. For a full-time, year-round worker, the minimum wage still leaves a family with one child almost $2000 below the poverty line.

As falling incomes have increased the need, government support for children has been gradually withdrawn. The real value of Aid for Families with Dependent Children (AFDC) has dropped by approximately 40% over 20 years. Today, less than 10% of all cash benefits go to poor families with children. Other groups have fared much better: over half of all people in poor families without children receive enough help to pull them above the poverty line - as opposed to only 14% of people in poor families with children.

Attempting to weight these factors, the report attributes just over 40% of the rise in child poverty to the decline of government support, just over 30% to falling real wages among the poor, and just under 30% to the rise of mother-only families.

Calling on the United States to use its resources to end child poverty by the year 2000, the CDF argues that "... *our high poverty rate is interfering with the healthy development and education of millions of our children and threatens the nation's economic and social future.*"

"*Eliminating child poverty*", on the other hand, "*would give the nation a huge running start on tackling the educational, health, substance abuse, crime, and other problems that seem so daunting.*"

And the cost? Money is by no means the only answer, but the CDF puts the bill at $28 billion a year (for raising every poor family with children up to the poverty line). This is less than 1% of America's GNP; it is also less than the amount received each year by the richest 1% of Americans as a result of additional tax breaks approved in the last 15 years.

Fig. 7 Spending on basics

Primary health care and primary education are two of the most important ways of 'investing in people'. But of 23 developing countries for which comparable figures are available, only three governments allocate more than one fifth of their expenditures to these basic services.

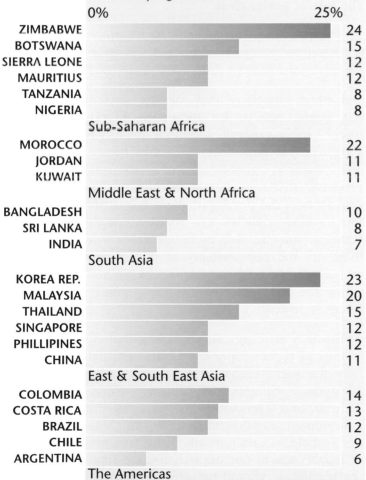

Expenditure on primary health care and primary and secondary education, as a percentage of total central government expenditures, selected developing countries, 1988

	0%	25%	
ZIMBABWE			24
BOTSWANA			15
SIERRA LEONE			12
MAURITIUS			12
TANZANIA			8
NIGERIA			8
Sub-Saharan Africa			
MOROCCO			22
JORDAN			11
KUWAIT			11
Middle East & North Africa			
BANGLADESH			10
SRI LANKA			8
INDIA			7
South Asia			
KOREA REP.			23
MALAYSIA			20
THAILAND			15
SINGAPORE			12
PHILLIPINES			12
CHINA			11
East & South East Asia			
COLOMBIA			14
COSTA RICA			13
BRAZIL			12
CHILE			9
ARGENTINA			6
The Americas			

Figures reflect only expenditures by central government and may therefore understate expenditures in countries with federal systems.
Source: UNDP,1991.

tries in Asia and Latin America have now passed through the earlier stages of this transition, when birth rates may or may not be affected, and are approaching or entering the stage during which further falls in child deaths could be expected to be associated with much steeper falls in births. In other words, reductions in child deaths have now reached the point where significant dividends in falling birth rates are likely to be paid out for any further reductions in child deaths that can be achieved. In Africa, where under-five mortality rates in most countries remain in the 150 to 250 band, it is essential to hasten this transition in order to quickly bring to a close the period during which population growth is at its most rapid.

"The effort to reduce child illness and malnutrition and to reach the goals of the World Summit for Children", says Maurice Strong, Secretary-General of the first *World Environment Conference* in Stockholm 20 years ago and of the *World Conference on Environment and Development* to be held in Rio de Janeiro in 1992, *"is crucial not only for its own sake but also as a means of helping to slow population growth and make possible environmentally sustainable development in the 21st century and beyond."*

A renewed commitment to protecting the health and the lives of the world's children is therefore in synergy with, not opposition to, the effort to cope with those other great issues on the human agenda for the 1990s - the slowing of population growth and the protection of the environment.

Investing in people

Proposition: *That the growing consensus around the importance of market economic policies should be accompanied by a corresponding consensus on the responsibility of governments to guarantee basic investments in people.*

Whether for idealistic or self-interested reasons, monopoly state control of economic life is an idea which has been given extensive field trials in the 20th century. But as that century ends, it is an idea whose time has gone. In particular, it stands discredited among the millions of people whose hopes it raised but whose needs it failed to meet.

The evidence of that failure is scattered not only over Eastern Europe and the Soviet Union but over even larger areas of the developing world. Free market economies, though facing many serious problems of their own, have generally shown themselves to be more successful in raising the living standards of the majority. It is therefore a truth now almost universally acknowledged that the energy and enterprise of peoples are liberated only when people are free to make their own decisions and mistakes and to reap rewards in relation to their labours.

The ideological chasms into which so much energy and commitment has disappeared in the post-war period are therefore narrowing to allow most countries to stand on the common ground of a market-friendly approach to development. This year's *World Development Report* from the World Bank, for example, marshals four decades of investment experience in support of this conclusion (panel 9). Similarly, the developing world's own review of progress, the recently published report of the *South Commission* chaired by former President Nyerere of Tanzania, has concluded, *"The successful examples of development in the South clearly show that economic growth is vigorous only in a climate in which the business sector can thrive."*[25]

The role of government

The role of government in development is therefore being re-evaluated in many nations at the present time.

Certain aspects of that role are obvious but ought not to be forgotten. Market forces cannot generate economic growth in a political vacuum. Durable peace, reasonable stability, guarantees of legal and property rights, a reasonably competent civil service, the development of infrastructure, sound policies on money supply, taxation, interest and exchange rates - all these are the responsibility of government and all are part of the framework without which the potential contribution of market forces is dissipated.

But it is also important to note that the lessons of recent experience - and particularly the successes of Hong Kong, Japan, Malaysia, Singapore, South Korea, Taiwan, and Thailand[26] - suggest not that government should retire from the economic field in order to allow the free play of market forces nor even that some single 'right balance' should be achieved between government and markets (which implies that the two must always be in opposition). The chief lesson is rather that progress is

Fig. 8 Arms, debt and people

About 40 percent of government spending in the developing world is devoted to the military and the servicing of debt. In some regions, this is twice as much as governments spend on health and education combined.

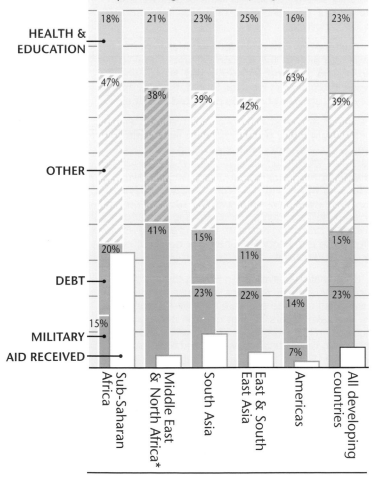

Percentage of central government expenditures (CGE) allocated to the military, debt servicing, health and education, and aid received as percentage of CGE, by region, 1988

* Includes Iran

Source: Based on World Bank, *World Debt Tables*, 1989/90 and *World Development Report*, 1991; IMF, *Government Finance Statistics Yearbook*, 1990; World Priorities Inc., *World Military and Social Expenditures*, 1991; OECD, *Development Co-operation, 1990 Report, and Financing and Central Debt of Developing Countries*, 1989 Survey.

most rapid when governments and markets work in intelligent partnership with each other.[27]

In the rethinking provoked by events in Eastern Europe and the Soviet Union, an equally clear if less widely proclaimed consensus is also emerging about what market forces cannot do, and therefore about what governments must do.

It is the responsibility of the state to:

○ Construct social safety nets to protect the most vulnerable members of society and set a minimum level of well-being which will be maintained even during economic downturns.

○ Ensure basic investments in people and especially in basic education and health care.

○ Promote full employment so that the great majority of citizens are able to meet their own and their families needs by their own efforts and their own earnings.

○ Counterbalance the long-term tendency of market forces to confer more opportunity on the already advantaged, thereby setting up a momentum towards increasing inequality.

○ Intervene in those instances where the free play of market forces is demonstrably counter to the public interest. From UNICEF's particular perspective, for example, it is not in the public interest to allow millions of children to become malnourished because the free play of market forces has persuaded millions of mothers to abandon breastfeeding in favour of commercial infant formulas (panel 12). Nor is it in the public interest for poor families the world

War on children: the 20th century's shame

6

Protecting the growing minds and bodies of young children should have first call on societies' concern in good times and in bad, in boom or recession, in peace or war. Entrenching that principle of 'first call' is the challenge of the 1990s. And nowhere is it more desperately needed than in the world's war zones.

In the last decade, more than one and a half million children have been killed in wars.[14] More than 4 million have been physically disabled - limbs amputated, brains damaged, eyesight and hearing lost - through bombing, land-mines, firearms, torture. Five million children are in refugee camps because of war; a further 12 million have lost their homes.

In 1991, this slaughter of the innocents continues in the more than 40 wars still being fought.

This 'war on children' is a 20th century invention. Only 5% of the casualties in the First World War were civilians. By the Second World War, the proportion had risen to 50%. And, as the century ends, the civilian share is normally about 80% - most of them women and children.

The indirect effects are almost as devastating. Schools and clinics are closed or destroyed. Food supply lines are broken. Water and sanitation systems break down. Millions flee to refugee camps. And always, the heaviest burden is borne by children - children who miss their one chance to grow normally in mind and body, to be educated and to acquire the skills to find a place in society.

The psychological wounds are less visible. In one study of 50 displaced children in Mozambique, 42 had lost a father or mother by violence, 11 had seen or heard a parent being killed, 29 had witnessed a murder, 16 had been kidnapped, all had been threatened or beaten or starved. The sample was said to be 'representative'.[15] In total, an estimated 10 million children in the world have suffered psychological trauma in civil and international wars.

These many millions of children, physically and mentally scarred by the conflicts of their elders, are part of the generation on which the future must be built.

The time has now come for a worldwide public to cry out against this war on children - against those who use the weapons and those who supply them. If wars must be fought, then, at the very least, children should be protected from their worst effects.

There are some signs of hope. Armed conflict seems to be lessening with the ending of the cold war. The *World Summit for Children* specifically called for the safeguarding of essential needs "*even in times of war and in violence-ridden areas*". And the new *Convention on the Rights of the Child*, which specifically demands "*all feasible measures to ensure protection and care of children who are affected by armed conflict*", has now been ratified by over 100 nations.

Some nations have begun putting the principle into practice. In El Salvador, civil war has been suspended on three separate days every year for the last seven years so that children can be immunized. In Lebanon, 'days of tranquillity' allowed children to be vaccinated even at the height of the troubles. In Sudan, both sides eventually agreed to 'corridors of peace', through which essential supplies could reach millions of civilians, mostly women and children, trapped in the war zone. Similar agreements have since been negotiated in Angola and Ethiopia. In Iraq, essential medical supplies were delivered even at the height of the Gulf conflict.

If such examples are to become the rule rather than the exception, worldwide public opinion will need to harden against the 'war on children' and insist that this appalling stain on the 20th century should not be allowed to seep over into the 21st.

over to be persuaded to spend $500 million a year on useless anti-diarrhoeal drugs when oral rehydration therapy, the medically correct treatment, is so low in cost that it is of little commercial interest.

○ Defend those elements of a humane and sustainable society to which the laws of the market place attach little or no value. This responsibility includes the protection of the environment, the protection of the future, and the defence of those who do not have sufficient influence or purchasing power to translate human need into economic or political demand.

Investing in people

The other half of the development consensus which has grown more solid as ideological divisions have narrowed is that it is a responsibility of governments to ensure that virtually all members of society have adequate nutrition, primary health care, clean water, safe sanitation, family planning services, and at least a primary education. These basic investments in people are essential not only for humanitarian reasons and for the creation of civilized societies but also as the foundations for sustained economic growth. As the outgoing President of the World Bank has said, in a letter to the Secretary-General of the United Nations following the *World Summit for Children*, *"Investment in human capital, including importantly basic health care and primary education for children, is one of the most effective means of stimulating long-term economic growth and improving general welfare."* The same conclusion was reached by the *South Commission's* review of recent

development experience which concluded: *"satisfying basic needs should have priority both on grounds of equity and to sustain economic growth at a rapid pace."*[28]

In recent years, research has demonstrated the power of that investment in many different ways. World Bank studies have shown that raising the average educational level of the labour force by one year can raise GDP by as much as 9%.[29] Other studies have demonstrated that four years of education, as opposed to none, can increase agricultural productivity by 10%.[30] Research over the years in Australia, Brazil, Colombia, Ethiopia, Guatemala, India, Indonesia, Kenya, and Sierra Leone have shown that improved nutrition can increase work productivity by up to 20%. Better adult and child health has been shown to save millions of lost workdays. Correcting child malnutrition and iron deficiency anaemia have been shown to reduce absenteeism, increase attention spans, and improve school results.[31]

But for the present purpose, such studies are like striking matches in daylight. The evidence that investing in people lays the foundations for economic growth looms large before us in the shape of those countries which have succeeded in achieving rapid and sustained progress in the postwar world. Liberating people's potential via land reforms and universal health and education services has been fundamental to that success in countries and regions such as Japan, South Korea, and Taiwan (panel 11). All of these have shown that basic education and health for all are not just social expenditures but economic investments, not just indulgences which can only be afforded after countries have

Ceara:
showing it can be done

Ceara is not a country. But with 6 million people, it is more populous than El Salvador or Costa Rica, Honduras or Nicaragua, Denmark or Norway.

In the three years from 1986 to 1989, Ceara has reduced its infant death rate by one third, cut child deaths from diarrhoeal diseases by half, boosted immunization levels by up to 40%, and reduced child malnutrition by one third. This impoverished state on the north-east coast of Brazil has therefore shown the world that the child health goals set for the year 2000 (page 61) can be achieved.

Ceara has no special advantages. Almost two thirds of its people live below the poverty line. But it does have the one essential advantage for improving the lives of children. Its leaders are personally and politically committed to the task. Given this commitment - in any country - the means now exist to revolutionize child health at an affordable cost.

Ceara's 1986 state elections brought to power a government including several people who had previously worked with UNICEF on local projects. Now, the chance had come to work together on a larger scale.

First, surveys drew up a picture of the 'state of Ceara's children' - revealing that infant mortality was running at 57 per 1,000 births, that the main causes of death were diarrhoeal diseases and pneumonia, and that 28% of all children were malnourished. Over half of all the children who died had never seen a health worker.

Next, a system was set up to monitor changes so that progress could be measured and resources targeted to where need was greatest.

Providing all families with basic health information, about such matters as the importance of breastfeeding, about the need for immunization, and about how to prevent and treat disease, was an obvious priority. But as in many other parts of the world, the health services did not have the means to reach out repeatedly to 6 million people. The state government therefore decided to appeal to the church, to the non-governmental organizations, to the mass media, to the business community (breastfeeding messages even appeared on bank statements), and to the Ceara Pediatrics Society. The commitment of the Catholic church was decisive, providing thousands of volunteers and reaching out to hundreds of thousands of people in the poorest areas of the state.

The drought of 1987, initially a set-back, was turned to advantage. Instead of the normal emergency employment programme, the government gave 6,000 'emergency jobs' to poor women who would be trained as community health workers. After the drought, 1,700 of the most promising were retrained. Their numbers have since grown to 2,900 - each looking after about 100 families. The Brazilian government now plans to employ 45,000 such health workers to extend the scheme to the nine states of the north-east.

The results of the programme are seen in fig. 9. Through both recession and drought, Ceara has put into practice the principle of 'first call for children'. It has not allowed the youngest and most vulnerable to take the brunt of adversity and has instead improved the protection given to the growing minds and bodies of the rising generation.

Life for the children of Ceara is not perfect. Child deaths remain too high. Primary health care is far from universal. And as many as half of all children leave school without even a basic education. But Ceara's commitment remains. The state government aims to meet all of the year 2000 goals adopted at the 1990 World Summit for Children.[16]

become prosperous but the foundations without which widespread prosperity will not be achieved.

In other words, the lessons of the last 40 years suggest that development proceeds most steadily when it walks on the two legs of a market-friendly economic policy and a government commitment to ensuring investment in people. And as the consensus on market-friendly economic policies visibly gathers momentum, it is even more essential that the other leg of the development consensus is also exercised.

Unfortunately, 'investing in people' has been the battle hymn of the international development effort for fifteen years without battle ever really being joined.

All for some

The governments of the developing countries spend, on average, about one quarter of their budgets on directly investing in people via health and education services (but not including government expenditures on agriculture and employment creation). Health and education together claim 17% of government expenditures in Latin America, 21% in the Middle East and North Africa, 23% in South Asia, and 25% in East and South East Asia (figs. 7 and 8).

In countries where high employment and reasonable wages mean that the majority are able to meet their own needs from their own earnings, such levels of social expenditure by governments might be adequate if allocated according to need. But of the sums which are allocated directly to health and education, more than half is allocated to relatively high cost services for the few, and less than half is allocated to low-cost services for the many (fig. 7). In other words, only about 12% of all government spending in the developing world is devoted to investing in the health and education of the poor majority.

Fig. 9 It can be done

The World Summit for Children set ambitious goals for the year 2000. But the Brazilian state of Ceara (population six million) has achieved some of the most basic goals in only three years (see panel 7).

Changes in selected maternal and child health indicators, Ceara, 1986-1989

Indicator	Oct/Dec 1986	Jun/Aug 1989	% change
Infant mortality	57	39	-32%
Infant mortality caused by diarrhoea (%)	28	13	-54%
Children given Oral Rehydration Salts in the last episode of diarrhoea (%)	23	32	+39%
Children 12-23 months receiving BCG vaccine (%)	58	81	+40%
Children 12-23 months receiving 3 doses of DPT vaccine (%)	50	63	+26%
Malnutrition – 2nd and 3rd grade by Gomez classification (%)	8.0	5.4	-33%

Unless otherwise stated, figures apply to children aged 0-36 months

Source: *Ceara, north east Brazil: giving priority to the child at the state level.* UNICEF Brazil, May 1991.

Reshuffling the pack: Human Development Report

8

The 1991 *Human Development Report* from UNDP is summed up by its own paraphrasing of Abraham Lincoln - '*development of the people, by the people, for the people*'. The liberation of peoples' potential and the widening of their participation and choice should be the aim of development. This will in turn stimulate economic growth. But economic growth is not an end in itself - it is a means by which further gains in human development may be achieved. Growth in national income is therefore necessary but not sufficient. What matters, too, is the kind of growth - what it consists of, how it is achieved, who benefits from it.

To measure progress towards this kind of development, UNDP proposes a *Human Development Index* or HDI, which ranks countries not just on economic or social performance but on a complex and composite scale which incorporates a modification of per capita GDP, average life expectancy, and years of schooling.

Humanizing the criteria of success in this way reshuffles the development pack. Algeria, for example, is placed 66th in the World Bank tables (which rank countries by per capita GNP) but slips to 102nd in the UNDP tables, which rank countries by their HDI. Conversely, Sri Lanka is ranked 120th by per capita GNP but promoted to 75th on the HDI because of its achievements in health and education.

The complex processes of human development, which must also include growing respect for human rights and political freedoms, is not the responsibility of government alone. But because the rights and the choices open to the majority can be widened or narrowed by how government allocates national revenues, UNDP suggests that government performance should be assessed by a set of linked ratios:

○ *the public expenditure ratio* - percentage of national income going into public expenditure (UNDP suggests about 25%)

○ *the social allocation ratio* - percentage of public expenditure allocated to social services like health and education (40% suggested)

○ *the social priority ratio* - percentage of social expenditure devoted to priority human needs such as primary health care and primary education (50% suggested).

The three ratios can be combined into one: a *human expenditure ratio* - the percentage of national income devoted to priority social concerns.

Applying these ratios to individual countries also produces interesting results. Zimbabwe, for example, has a *human expenditure ratio* of 12.7, and Pakistan only 0.8. But even countries with the same overall ratio can arrive there by different routes. India and Thailand both have *human expenditure ratios* of 2.5% even though their *public expenditure ratios* are very different - 37% and 16% respectively. Thailand makes up for having lower public spending by having higher social allocation and social priority ratios.

The report suggests an *aid human expenditure ratio* (the proportion of a donor's GNP allocated to human priority needs in the developing world). Applied to present aid programmes, this ratio varies from a high of 0.128% in the Netherlands and 0.110% in Denmark, to a low of 0.012% in the United States and 0.017% in Italy.

In recent years, UNICEF has used slightly different concepts, asking, first, what proportion of government spending goes to basic human needs such as primary health care, primary education, and low-cost water supply and, second, what proportion of aid is used to directly meet such needs (figs. 11 and 12).

Such analyses show that many countries are in a stronger position to accelerate human development than their economic position might suggest. Some countries have clearly achieved much more with much less. Others have shown that even when public expenditure has to be cut, reordering priorities can still allow progress.

It is estimated, for example, that 80% of the $12 billion allocated each year to water supply systems is spent on putting private taps in the homes of the relatively well-off, at a cost of approximately $600 per person served, and that only 20% goes to the public wells and stand-pipes which can bring clean water to the poor majority at a cost of $30 to $50 per person served.[32] Reallocating even a proportion of total expenditures in favour of the poor could therefore liberate enough resources to achieve the goal of safe water supply for almost every community in almost every country by the year 2000.

A similar argument, with similar statistics, could be built around the theme of health care. For many times more money to be spent on curative than on preventive health is the norm; for 75% of public spending on health to serve only the richest 25% of the population is not untypical;[33] for more to be spent on sophisticated operations than on the low-cost control of mass disease is not uncommon;[34] for 30% of health budgets to be spent on sending a privileged few for treatment abroad is not unknown.[35]

The necessary restructuring of such expenditures may be difficult but it is not impossible. On becoming independent, for example, Bangladesh found itself with a health system which devoted only 10% of its expenditure to rural health clinics serving the great majority of its population. Today, that figure has been raised to 60%.[36]

Education

Such distortions of public spending in favour of the better-off are also evident in national education systems.

Despite decades of research findings which regularly demonstrate that investment in *primary* education yields significantly higher returns in both social progress end economic growth,[37] government spending in almost all developing countries is heavily biased towards higher education for the few rather than basic education for the many.

This is not the path that has been followed by those countries which have achieved the mutually reinforcing goals of universal education and sustained economic growth. In both Japan and South Korea, for example, universal primary education preceded economic take-off. And in both, this basic investment in people was made at a stage when their per capita incomes, in real terms, were lower than in most developing countries today. Japan moved rapidly towards universal primary education at the end of the last century. South Korea ensured that almost all its children were in primary school at a stage when its per capita GNP was little more than $100 per year (panel 11). Emphasis on secondary and higher education came later and was not made at the expense of primary education for the great majority. Nor did it run very far ahead of the economy's capacity to absorb increasing numbers of more highly educated people.

Many other countries have taken the opposite course, financing higher education disproportionately with the result that up to half of all children fail to complete four years in primary school while secondary and tertiary education absorbs an exaggerated share of the budget in order to produce many more graduates than the economy can usefully absorb. In India, where between 60 and 70 children could be given primary education for the cost of training one university student,[38] approximately half of the nation's children fail to finish primary school while the country as a whole produces more graduates than it can productively employ. Inevitably, one of the effects is a brain drain of unemployed but highly qualified people to the industrialized nations. In this way, a significant share of government spending on education is used to subsidize the rich nations rather than to achieve basic education for all which, as all experience suggests, is one of the cornerstones of development.

For reasons of both justice and efficiency, the overall effect of educational expenditure should be to redistribute incomes and equalize opportunities. In most developing countries today, its effect is almost the opposite. Most government spending on higher education is spending on the already advantaged; in Chile, the Dominican Republic, and Uruguay, for example, more than 50% of all government spending on higher education is devoted to the children of families who belong to the richest 20% of the population. In India, 50% of all government spending on education is used to subsidize the best-educated 10%.[39]

Within these inequities lies the potential for a degree of restructuring of educational expenditures which could help to finance progress towards the goal of access to basic education for all children (and the completion of primary school by at least 80%) before the year 2000.

If that goal is to be met, then an extraordinary effort is called for in the early 1990s. In particular, low-cost ways and means will have to be found of retaining or returning those who now drop out of school in the first year or two of formal education. Considerable progress has been made in enrolling children in school; the more difficult problem is that up to half of those who do enrol leave before becoming literate (fig. 10 and panel 10). Those children are essentially being locked out of the 21st century.

Pioneering efforts in Bangladesh,[40] Colombia, Zimbabwe, and in many other countries in recent years, have shown that access to a basic education for all children, and completion of primary school for the great majority, can be achieved at an affordable cost. Using such new methods, the extra financial cost of reaching these goals can be estimated at approximately $5 billion a year throughout the 1990s. The costs of not achieving that goal will be far higher. World Bank research over the last 10 years has demonstrated many times that *"the productivity of an educated work force is the most reliable engine of economic growth."*[41] But the investment in education yields its dividends in many other forms. It confers the ability to continue learning, from a wide range of sources, throughout adult life. It modernizes attitudes[42] and builds confidence in change. It stimulates broader participation in political life. It assists the process of allowing what is good in the new to replace what is bad in the old. It brings an awareness of new ideas and new choices. It raises the average age of marriage, makes family planning more likely, and reduces

Fig. 10 Disappearing pupils

Over 90 percent of children now start school in the developing world. But millions do not even reach the fourth grade. Most are lost in the first year or two.

Survival rates in primary school, by region, 1986-1989

Percentage of those starting primary school who reach grades 2 ⊙ , 3 ⊙ , and 4 ⊙

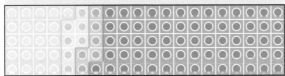

SUB SAHARAN AFRICA
Reaching grades 2 = 79% 3 = 72% 4 = 66%

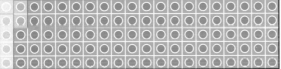

ARAB STATES
Reaching grades 2 = 99% 3 = 95% 4 = 93%

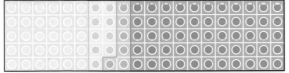

LATIN AMERICA AND THE CARIBBEAN
Reaching grades 2 = 70% 3 = 61% 4 = 55%

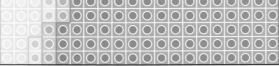

EASTERN ASIA
Reaching grades 2 = 87% 3 = 83% 4 = 78%

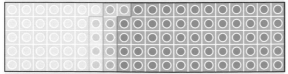

SOUTHERN ASIA
Reaching grades 2 = 69% 3 = 65% 4 = 59%

Source: Basic education and literacy, world statistical indicators, UNESCO, 1990.

birth rates. As Japan's Prime Minister, Toshiki Kaifu, told the assembled heads of state at the *World Summit for Children* : *"It is no exaggeration to say that the policy of promoting education constituted the very foundation of Japan's development. In developing countries the first priority should be to institute and improve basic education and raise the literacy rate among children so as to enable them to live with dignity. National development can take place only when all people have the opportunity to receive education."*

Lower cost

In addition to economic growth in the developing world or increased aid from the industrialized nations, both of which are to be hoped for in the 1990s, the resources for investing in people might come from three other sources. The first is some degree of restructuring of government spending in the developing world to shift resources in favour of low-cost services for the many rather than high-cost services for the few. In many countries, for example, even a relatively modest shift in this direction would be enough to invest in a basic education for all. The second possible source is a similar restructuring of existing aid programmes in order to devote a larger proportion to the task of investing in people's health and education. That notion is the subject of the next chapter of this report. The third possibility would be to take full advantage of the fact that the greater knowledge, technology, and communications capacity now available holds out the clear possibility of investing in the health, nutrition, and education of the rising generation at a much lower cost than

Reducing poverty: World Development Report

9

The 1980 *World Development Report* became a landmark. In its pages, the World Bank demonstrated that the worst symptoms of poverty - mass malnutrition, illiteracy, ill health - could be overcome by direct government action and that the countries which achieved this were also likely to achieve higher rates of economic growth.

In the decade since then, the annual *World Development Report* has dwelled more on the purely economic policies which the Bank considers a help or a hindrance to growth.

In its 1991 report, the Bank returns to the theme of direct poverty reduction, arguing for education and health services and employment creation programmes. "*Investing in people*", says the report, "*makes sense not just in human terms but in hard-headed economic terms*". The well-known examples of Japan and the Republic of Korea are cited. And as in 1980, when the Bank showed that farmers with even four years of primary education were significantly more productive, the 1991 report quotes studies from India and the Philippines to show that better-nourished children grow up to be not just healthier but higher-earning adults.

The 1991 *World Development Report* therefore contributes to the confluence of opinion that economic growth and human well-being should be pursued simultaneously and that the two are mutually reinforcing. But it sticks closely to the view that government's place is in the arena of social investment rather than economic management. 'Maximum investment in people and minimum intervention in markets' is the nub of the Bank's current advice.

To demonstrate the synergism between these two dicta, the report compares the growth record of individual developing countries with their conformity to this advice over the last 20 years. Taking price distortions as a measure of 'market interference' and education as a measure of 'investment in people', the Bank concludes that countries that did badly on both criteria grew, on average, by 3.1% a year. The countries which did well on only one criterion only (regardless of which one) grew by 3.8% a year. But those countries wise enough to anticipate the Bank's advice and perform well against both criteria, had a much more impressive growth rate of 5.5% a year. In other words, the whole adds up to considerably more than the sum of its parts.

Yet the Bank is not even-handed in its scrutiny of these two aspects of development policy. Its implication continues to be that markets can do little wrong and that all economic growth is necessarily to the good (including the kind of growth which the World Bank has assisted in the Amazon region and which has benefited neither the poor majority or the environment). Government intervention in the economy, on the other hand, is always regarded as guilty until proven innocent.

This is at odds with the pragmatism which the Bank now advocates, and the contradiction occasionally surfaces. As a new study[17] points out, and as the Bank itself acknowledges, the state has had a heavy hand in the most successful economies of the last 40 years. In Hong Kong, Japan, the Republic of Korea, Singapore and Taiwan governments have harnessed private enterprise to an overall development strategy. They have, for example, enacted fundamental land reforms, protected domestic producers, promoted selected industries, and discriminated against property and financial holdings in favour of industrial assets. But as the Bank rightly points out, their governments have, in general, avoided the two crucial mistakes; they have not allowed heavy distortions of prices and exchange rates; and they have not allowed interventionist policies to be captured and strait-jacketed by vested interests.

has previously been thought possible (see, for example panels 5 and 16). Put in another way, the gap between the experience and technology now available and its large-scale application is an opportunity to wring considerable social and economic returns from relatively small investments.

The year 2000 goals adopted at the *World Summit for Children* reflect these low-cost opportunities and represent a practical programme, with a significant political commitment behind it, for 'investing in people' over the next decade. That programme, adapted to national needs and supported by the international community, should become the essential complement to the economic reforms that are now beginning in many countries of the developing world.

Aid and need

Proposition: *That increases in international aid should be based on a sustained and measurable commitment to meeting minimum human needs and for maintaining, in difficult times, the principle of a first call for children.*

The public in the industrialized world has long believed that the great majority of the aid it gives to the developing world is spent on directly meeting the basic needs of the poor. In fact, the proportion of the industrialized world's aid that is used for such purposes is only 10% to 15% (figs. 11 and 12).

If aid to secondary education, as opposed to primary, is excluded, then that proportion drops to below 5%. Only about 1% of international aid goes to the primary health care systems which could prevent or treat 80% of the disease, malnutrition, and early deaths in the developing world. Only about 1% goes to the family planning services which could do so much to improve the lives of millions of women and children (see pages 58 to 60). And considerably less than 1% goes to primary education[43] which, as we have seen, is both a basic human need and one of the best possible investments that any country can make in its own future.

If a renewed effort to end absolute poverty is to be a part of a new world order, then the proportion of international aid which is devoted directly to this task must rise significantly over the next few years.

The final declaration adopted at the *World Summit for Children* called on the industrialized nations to review present aid budgets in the light of the goals adopted. National programmes of action, which most industrialized countries are preparing as a follow-up to the *Summit,* will not be available until after this report is published, but several donor countries are known to be seeking to increase their allocations to programmes which will help to achieve the year 2000 goals. In the United States, Congress has made funding appropriations in fiscal 1992 totalling some $500 million for international follow-up on the commitments made at the *World Summit for Children* and much larger appropriations for domestic programmes. In Australia, aid allocations are being examined with a view to shifting the balance in favour of programmes which support the Summit goals. In Norway, a white paper will be submitted to parliament on this subject late in 1991. In Germany, an all-party agreement in the *Bundestag* has committed the Development Ministry to the policy that poverty alleviation, with the participation of the poor themselves, will be the central purpose of the aid programme. Switzerland, Canada, and the Netherlands have all taken initiatives towards debt-relief for the specific purpose of programmes to benefit children and accelerate progress towards the *Summit* goals.

Purpose of aid

Aid which is allocated to meeting the basic needs of the poor, and particularly to the nutrition, health, and education of the children, would receive growing support from the public in the industrialized nations. All the evidence, most recently from a major survey of public opinion in Australia,[44] suggests that many would march in the cause of abolishing mass malnutrition, preventable ill-health, and widespread illiteracy among the world's children.

It is especially important, at this time, that this concern is expressed and that the non-governmental organizations and the concerned public in the industrialized nations should also mobilize behind the commitments made and the goals agreed at the *Summit for Children*. And one of the most important ways in which that public can contribute towards the achievement of those goals is through increasing the pressure for aid to be used for investing in children.

The particular importance of this potential contribution from the industrialized world lies in the fact that many of the proposals discussed in this report, and many of the goals adopted at the *World Summit for Children*, have a fundamental political weakness. In many cases, they are asking governments to give priority to long-term needs or to the poorest and least influential sectors of society. It is often difficult for governments, confronted by short-term pressures and powerful vested interests, to adopt changes whose political or economic benefits are often not visible above the electoral horizon. Making international aid available specifically to finance such changes is one of the very few ways of helping to compensate for this inherent weakness. With sufficient public commitment in the industrialized nations, aid could fulfil the specific role of boosting the political attractiveness of programmes whose

Fig. 11 Where aid goes

Only about 15 percent of all aid goes to health and education (all levels) and to population programmes. Only about 2 percent goes to primary health care and primary education which are the most fundamental services for the poor majority of the developing world.

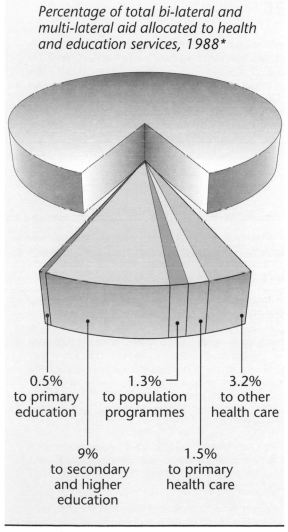

Percentage of total bi-lateral and multi-lateral aid allocated to health and education services, 1988*

0.5%
to primary
education

1.3%
to population
programmes

3.2%
to other
health care

9%
to secondary
and higher
education

1.5%
to primary
health care

* This figure differs from figure 12 in including all donor countries, all levels of health care, multi-lateral as well as bi-lateral aid programmes, and in using World Bank data as well as OECD data (and for 1988 rather than 1989). Problems of definition and incompatibilities of reporting method mean that figures are approximate only.

Source: Derived from OECD (1989) and World Bank (1991).

principal beneficiaries would be the people and the causes with the least political leverage - the poor, the uninfluential, the future, and the environment.

Aid could, for example, be used to ease the frictions that would inevitably be involved in the restructuring of government expenditures discussed in chapter the previous chapter. The principal difficulty in shifting social expenditures in favour of the poor majority is usually a political one; increasing the proportion of the budget spent on primary health care or primary education represents, in effect, a transfer of resources from the better-off and the politically influential to the poor and the powerless. Where affluence is inseparable from influence, that transition will be very difficult indeed. Under the increasing number of democratic systems, in which the greater numbers of the voting poor give them a degree of political leverage, the transition will be easier. But even where governments are willing to restructure budgets in favour of the poor majority, they are often inhibited from doing so by the pressure of entrenched vested interests. Aid that is made available specifically for the purpose of investing in primary health care or primary education, for example, could mean that the rebalancing of allocations internally is made politically easier. And it is in the easing of such political obstacles to essential change that the support of the international community could play a particular and vital role in the years ahead.

Similarly, aid could help to maintain the principle of first call for children (page 15).

Education: school staying power

10

The 1980s was a disastrous decade for education. Out of over 100 developing countries surveyed by UNESCO, two thirds saw a decline in expenditures per pupil and half saw a fall in the proportion of their children enrolled in primary school.[18]

The cause, in most cases, was the cut in public spending forced on many countries by the debt crisis. The consequence is that millions of children, especially in Africa and Latin America, have lost their opportunity to become literate and to acquire the basic skills necessary to themselves and their societies in the years ahead.

Africa has been hit particularly hard. Total educational expenditure was cut by almost 30% in the first half of the 1980s. As a result, the proportion of Africa's children enrolled in the first year of primary school fell from 84% in 1980 to approximately 70% in 1990.[19]

Debt was not the only cause. Educational policies and international aid programmes could have done more to protect primary education. But too often, available resources have been devoted to higher education for the few rather than basic education for the many.

Even though 50 or more children can be provided with primary education for the cost of one university student,[20] and even though thousands of university graduates must choose between unemployment and emigration, many countries continue to devote disproportionate resources to higher education.[21] A relatively small shift in this balance could, in many cases, achieve universal primary education and produce much greater national benefits in both economic growth and social progress.

Aid programmes have reinforced the bias. Less than 10% of aid goes to education and less than 5% of this goes to *primary* education.[22] The 1990 *World Summit for Children* set the target of achieving a basic level of education for at least 80% of children by the year 2000. That goal can be met, as the extraordinary achievements of Tanzania in the 1970s and Zimbabwe in the 1980s have shown. The example of the BRAC schools in Bangladesh has also demonstrated that it is possible, at very low cost, to provide a basic education to those children (and especially girls) who have dropped out of, or never started in, the official primary school system.[23] Most of the children attending the BRAC schools later rejoin formal education.

But to achieve the year 2000 goal, primary education will have to assume a new priority in the years immediately ahead.

The task is not primarily one of building new schools and training new teachers. It is the *quality* of the education on offer which will determine success or failure in the 1990s.[24]

Enrolment in the first year of primary school has already reached high levels in all regions of the developing world except Africa.[25] The physical capacity to accommodate all children is therefore not the principal problem. It is enrolment in the *final* year of primary school which counts. And of the relevant age group in each continent, final year primary school enrolment is still only 47% in Africa, 53% in Asia (not including China) and 64% in Latin America.[26]

In other words, the great majority of uneducated children in the 1990s will be uneducated not because they did not go to school but because they did not stay there.

Apart from poverty and the need for children's help at home and at work, the main reason for these debilitating drop-out rates is the poor quality of the education provided. In too many cases, the relevance and standard of the education on offer is so obviously poor that, as a recent UNESCO report puts, "*parents and pupils have no other rational choice than to vote with their feet*".[27]

That principle implies protecting the long-term interests of children against even the most intense short-term pressures for spending cuts in nutrition programmes, primary health services, or primary education. In the same way, many of the actions needed to protect the environment and achieve sustainable development also require a commitment to the long term which most governments, hard-pressed by short-term considerations, find difficult to make. Aid can make that commitment more politically feasible. Similar arguments apply, in varying degrees, to such essential investments in people as primary health care services, basic education, land reforms, advancing female equality, or restructuring government budgets in favour of basic services for the poor.

In other words, the essence of this proposal is that, in a new world order, international aid should be consciously and specifically used to help prevent the important from being subverted by the immediate.

Public support

The use of aid in this way would need to be worked out in partnership with the receiving nations. Its potential should not be dissipated by unreasonable attitudes towards 'conditionality' on either side. Without the support of politicians, press, and public in the industrialized world, there will be no significant increase in aid in the years ahead. That support will not be forthcoming without regard to the purposes which aid serves. The necessary increases in international aid will therefore depend on a sustained and demonstrable commitment, on the part of aid donors and aid receivers, to the task of enhancing the capacity of the poorest, their health and nutrition, their education and training, their ability to exert more control over their own lives, and to earn a fair reward for their labours, and to meet their own and their families' needs. Aid that fulfils that purpose is the kind of aid which the majority of people in the developing world want to receive and kind of aid which the majority of people in the industrialized world want to give.

The economic environment

Proposition: *That international action on debt, aid, and trade should create an environment in which economic reform in the developing world can succeed in allowing its people to earn a decent living.*

Although average incomes have risen substantially in Asia (including China and India), the 1980s were nonetheless a disastrous decade for the majority of countries in the developing world. Average incomes fell by approximately 10% in Latin America (and by much more among the poorest) and by 25% in Africa (where incomes were already the lowest in the world).[45]

In 1990, this uneven pattern has continued. In the 18 countries of East Asia, per capita incomes rose by over 4% in 1990; in the eight countries of South Asia (including Bangladesh, India, and Pakistan) per capita incomes rose by just over 2%. But in the two most debt-ridden continents, the decline of the 1980s has continued; per capita incomes fell again by over 2% in Africa and by over 2.5% in Latin America (and even more steeply in countries such as Argentina, Brazil, and Peru, which have extremely high levels of debt).[46]

The economic environment within which the developing world must earn its living is not the primary responsibility of those organizations and individuals who work directly with the problems of children. But for a decade UNICEF has watched the deterioration of that economic environment being translated, in many countries, into rising malnutrition, preventable disease, and falling school enrolments. Proposals to reverse this deterioration would therefore have an air of unreality if they failed to also acknowledge the enormous economic difficulties under which so many countries are still labouring.

It is particularly important to address those difficulties at the present time. Shaken into a new realism by the harsh economic ride of the 1980s, and aware of the experience of Central and Eastern Europe, many if not most developing nations have begun to adopt the kind of economic reforms that could bring increasing prosperity to their peoples in the years ahead. This change in attitude and economic thinking has passed almost unnoticed in a world preoccupied by more dazzling change (although some commentators have noted that these changes represent a *"quiet revolution"* with a *"potential for advancing human welfare that can scarcely be exaggerated".*[47]) But it is an opportunity not to be missed.

At the moment, it is unlikely that this potential will be fulfilled because too many of the factors which brought disaster in the 1980s are still present in the 1990s. Even if economic policy and management were to improve, the problems of external debt, of declining terms of trade, of protectionism in the rich world's markets, and of excessive military spending, still remain. In other words, the developing world will find it difficult to find a place in a new world order because it is still chained to the mistakes of the old.

World prices for raw materials, on which so many developing countries are dependent, remain at their lowest levels since the depression of the 1930s. In the last decade alone, the price that Africa is paid for its primary products has fallen by approximately 30% in relation to the price it has to pay for its imports.

The degree of dependence on such commodities, and the steady deterioration in their real value, is one of development's most intransigent problems. And it is going to get worse. As new technologies, synthetics, and management systems continue to increase manufacturing efficiency, fewer raw materials will be needed. And in the years ahead, the increasing use of biotechnology could further undermine the trading position of agricultural raw materials.

It seems that there is little the developing world can do to prevent this steady erosion of its prices and markets. It can attempt to coordinate production, at least regionally, to avoid depressing prices further by overproduction. It can also attempt to strengthen its own research and development capacity for processing more of its own raw materials into semi-manufactured or manufactured goods. But at the same time, it must attempt to diversify its exports to reduce its dependence on a crumbling economic base.

The problem with diversification of exports is that the industrialized world, which so enthusiastically urges free market policies on the developing world, protects its own producers by surrounding itself with tariffs, quotas, and subsidies which effectively close the rich world's markets to a whole range of possible exports from the developing world (including a wide range of agricultural and tropical produce, steel, textiles, clothing, leather goods and footwear).

Estimates of the cost of such protectionism to the developing world vary widely, but the total is not less than $55 billion a year[48] - more than all the aid received. A dismantling of those tariff and non-tariff barriers would, according to IMF managing director, Michel Camdessus, raise the growth rate of developing countries by nearly 3 percentage points, so yielding benefits equal to twice the aid they receive.[49]

Fig. 12 Aid for basics

The twelve industrialized countries for which information is available give about 9 percent of their aid to directly meeting the most basic needs of people in the developing world.

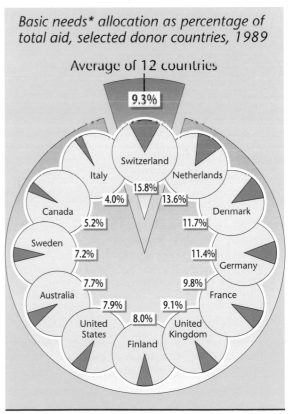

Basic needs* allocation as percentage of total aid, selected donor countries, 1989

Average of 12 countries

9.3%

Switzerland 15.8%
Italy 4.0%
Netherlands 13.6%
Canada 5.2%
Denmark 11.7%
Sweden 7.2%
Germany 11.4%
Australia 7.7%
France 9.8%
United States 7.9%
Finland 8.0%
United Kingdom 9.1%

* 'Basic needs spending' is defined here as expenditures on primary health care, primary and secondary education, family planning, and rural water supply and sanitation.
Source: OECD and UNDP, 1991.

South Korea: more education per dollar

11

The most obvious common denominator of the Asian success stories - Hong Kong, Japan, the Republic of Singapore, South Korea, Taiwan - is not the wealth of their natural resources but the wealth of their human resources. From the earliest stages of economic development, all of them invested heavily in education.[1]

In the early 1950s, few would have backed South Korea as the star economic performer of the second half of the century. It has few natural resources and little fertile land. Worse, its immediate history included 36 years of Japanese colonialism followed by devastation in the Korean war.

Yet by the mid-1950s, educational levels were running two or three times higher than could be expected for a country with a GNP of only $90 per capita. And by 1960, just before the country's economic take-off, 90% of children were completing primary school and over one third were going on to secondary education.

In the three decades since then, South Korea's economy has grown by 7% a year - faster than almost any other nation.

Two features make South Korea's achievement unique. First, it universalized primary education at an earlier stage in its economic development than practically any other country. Second, it did so with relatively little investment by government. For 30 years, spending on education never exceeded 3% of GNP - less than the average for the developing world.

In short, South Korea succeeded in wringing more education out of every government dollar than any other country. How was it achieved?

First, government both encouraged and depended on a massive social demand for education which translated into a willingness of parents to pay. From 1950 to 1975, students and their families picked up approximately 50% of the educational bill.

In part, this willingness to make sacrifices comes from a 2,000 year-old Confucian tradition of respect for the educated person. In part also, it is born of the more worldly perception that economic and social status is determined more by education than by anything else.

Second, Korean policy subsidized education less and less at each successive level, devoting most of its resources to ensuring primary education for all and letting the private sector pick up an increasing share of the bill for secondary and higher education. Even so, 25% of the cost of primary education was initially met by parents, through 'voluntary' parent-teacher association contributions.

Third, high class sizes and low teacher salaries have kept the cost of education lower than in almost any other developing country. For 30 years, the average number in a primary class remained at around 55. This was made manageable by rote-learning, rigid syllabuses, and strict examination requirements. School life verged on the paramilitary, with mass calisthenics, marching to music, and bowing to teachers. Teachers did not have to worry about discipline, and they were compensated for low salaries by high status.

Fourth, South Korea decided on a system of automatically promoting pupils from one grade to the next. In many developing countries, much primary school capacity is devoted to 'repeaters' and to those who drop out after a year or two. In South Korea, there are almost no repeaters or drop-outs. All students are expected to progress. Failure to do so is put down to lack of application rather than lack of ability.

Finally, parental pressure to pass examinations has led to the widespread practice of *yuksonghoe* - paying for extra tuition. This raises levels of educational achievement and supplements teachers' salaries while costing the state nothing.[28]

Dismantling such trade barriers, through a successful completion of the present Uruguay round of talks under the General Agreement on Tariffs and Trade, would therefore provide much needed oxygen to the process of economic reform in the developing world.

Debt

In addition to these problems, many developing nations are prevented from moving forward and taking their place in any new world order because they are held back by the seemingly immovable weight of their debt.

In total, the developing world owes approximately $1,300 billion to the governments and banks of the industrialized nations and to international financial institutions. Each year, the repayment of capital and interest amounts to approximately $150 billion - roughly three times as much as the developing world receives in aid. As it is impossible to meet those interest charges in full, the amount unpaid is added to the total debt owed. In this way, the debt burden has gathered its own momentum which has taken it to the point where not only can the debt never be repaid but the attempt to meet even the interest charges is often crippling to the movement towards economic reform.

So far, the industrialized world's role in the debt crisis has not been a virtuous one. First, irresponsible lending is as much to blame as irresponsible borrowing. Second, it is not acting in good faith to urge developing countries to earn their way out of the crisis by diversifying and exporting more while at the same time maintaining tariff and other trade barriers which prevent the developing world from successfully following this advice. Third, the laws covering individual bankruptcy and debt in most industrial countries set limits on creditors, not allowing so much to be reclaimed as to leave the debtor unable to feed his or her family or even to afford the means of earning a living; it is time that this concept was applied to international transactions.

To move forward, the developing world desperately needs to invest in its infrastructure, its industrialization, and its people. When its raw materials earnings are in decline, when the interest on its debts absorbs a quarter of all its earnings, and when new export markets are closed by protectionism, then these essential investments in the future simply cannot be made.

For several decades, the developing world has also been able to count on aid and concessional finance for at least a part of the investment it needs. But the debt crisis has now reached such a point of absurdity that the developing nations are having to transfer financial resources to the industrialized nations rather than the other way round. When all transactions are taken into account - the amount that all sources in the industrialized nations lend to the developing countries minus the amounts that the developing countries pay back in repayments of capital and interest - the net effect is that the developing world is now transferring $40 to $50 billion a year to the industrialized world (fig. 13).

It will not be easy to reverse this financial flow in the early 1990s when investment finance is likely to be in short supply. The

Baby-friendly hospitals: a million lives to save

12

Five years from now, thousands of hospitals throughout the world could have a plaque by the front entrance designating them as 'baby-friendly'. The idea is the latest advance in a decade-long campaign to counter the worldwide trend towards bottle-feeding.

Breastmilk is more nutritious, more hygienic, cheaper, immunizes against common infections, protects mothers against pregnancy and reduces the risk of breast and ovarian cancer.[29]

Despite all this, breastfeeding has declined as more families move to towns, more mothers go out to work, more hospitals discourage breastfeeding, and more advertisements suggest that bottle-feeding is the modern way.

Apart from being inferior in quality, powdered milk is often over-diluted with unclean water in unsterile bottles. So a bottle-fed baby in a poor community is approximately 15 times more likely to die from diarrhoeal disease and 4 times more likely to die from pneumonia than a baby who is exclusively breastfed.[30] Overall, WHO estimates that more than a million children's lives could be saved every year if all mothers gave their babies nothing but breastmilk for the first four to six months of life.

Ten years ago, WHO and UNICEF drew up a 'code of practice' for the marketing of breastmilk substitutes. The code sought to ban all public advertising and all supplies of free infant formula.

Now, the two organizations have also drawn up a code of practice for the hospitals themselves. What nurses do in hospitals sets a powerful example to millions of mothers. And what happens in the first few hours after birth can decide whether or not a mother will successfully breastfeed. But in many hospitals today, newborns are kept in separate rooms and given a bottle of infant formula soon after birth. Hospitals and mothers are often given free samples in order to promote a particular brand of infant formula.

The new code sets out 'Ten Steps to Successful Breastfeeding'.[31] All hospitals following the code will be designated 'baby-friendly'. The 10 steps are:

1. have a written breastfeeding policy - routinely communicated to all health staff

2. train all health staff in skills to implement this policy

3. inform all pregnant women about the benefits and management of breastfeeding

4. help mothers initiate breastfeeding within half an hour of birth

5. show mothers how to breastfeed, and how to maintain lactation even if they should be separated from their infants

6. give newborn infants no food or drink other than breastmilk, unless *medically* indicated

7. practise rooming-in (allow mothers and infants to remain together) 24 hours a day

8. encourage breastfeeding on demand

9. give no artificial teats or pacifiers (also called dummies or soothers) to breastfeeding infants

10. foster the establishment of breastfeeding support groups and refer mothers to them on discharge from the hospital or clinic.

Many women in the developing world do not give birth in hospitals. Those who do usually stay there for only 48 hours. So the worldwide 'baby-friendly hospitals' campaign, launched by UNICEF and WHO in Ankara in mid-1991,[32] can only be one step among many needed to promote breastfeeding. Mothers need the support of hospitals if they are to give their babies the best possible start; but if they are to continue breastfeeding, they will also need the support of employers, trade unions, communities - and of men.

While pressing ahead with the baby-friendly hospital idea, UNICEF and WHO are also calling on the infant formula companies, who have responded positively, to stop all free and subsidized distribution to maternity wards and hospitals before the end of 1992.

Soviet Union, several of its Republics, and the nations of Eastern Europe will all absorb vast amounts of investment capital. At the same time, reconstruction costs in Kuwait and Iraq are estimated at between $150 and $300 billion.[50] But only by a more drastic resolution of the debt crisis than any so far proposed, and a reversal of net financial transfers to the developing world, can much of the developing world hope to regain the ground lost in the last decade.

If the ways and means can be found to cut nations free from this leaden legacy, then the economic reforms now in evidence could coincide with other favourable circumstances to allow an unprecedented period of growth. As the World Bank's review of prospects for development in the 1990s has said: *"The opportunity for rapid development is greater today than at any time in history. International links, in the form of trade and flows of information, investment and technology, are stronger now than forty years ago. Medicine, science, and engineering have all made great strides; the benefits are available world-wide. And policy makers have a better understanding than before of the options for development."*[51]

Disarmament

Proposition: *That a process of demilitarization should begin in the developing world and that, in step with that process, falling military expenditures in the industrialized nations should be linked to significant increases in international aid for development and for the resolution of common global problems.*

Military spending in the developing world, although varying widely from region to region, is running at approximately $150 billion a year.[52] In Africa, a continent still desperately poor and desperately in need of diversifying and industrializing its economies, one third of all the machinery imported each year is destined for the military. In the developing world as a whole, just the import of armaments absorbs an amount equivalent to 75% of all the aid received.[53] In general, it is in the very poorest countries where spending on the military is highest (fig. 14). The 46 least developed countries - the poorest group of countries in the world - spend as much on their military capacity as on health and education combined.

The true costs of this massive military spending, year after year, go beyond the destruction of war (panel 6) and the diversion of scarce resources. Stimulated and sustained by superpower rivalries, a

China:
reaching 90%

13

After an extraordinary effort in the 1980s, the target of immunizing 80% of the world's children by their first birthdays has been reached by most countries. But it is not enough. Immunization levels will have to rise further if disease transmission is to be disrupted, if measles deaths are to fall by the aimed-for 95%, if polio is to be eradicated, if neonatal tetanus is to be eliminated, and if the poorest and most vulnerable children are to be protected. That is why the *World Summit for Children* adopted the new target of 90% immunization coverage in all countries by the year 2000.

Reaching and sustaining the extra 10% will prove almost as big a task for the 1990s as reaching 80% was to the 1980s. But its feasibility has already been demonstrated in the world's most populous nation.

In 1985, China set itself the target of reaching 85% of all children - in the nation as a whole by 1988, in every province by 1989, and in every county by 1990. Today immunization coverage in China stands at 99% for BCG vaccine, 98% for the three doses of polio vaccine, 97% for the three doses of DPT, and 98% for the single measles shot. The results are already evident in a steep fall in vaccine-preventable disease. The number of measles cases, for example, has dropped from over 2 million a year to less than 100,000. Polio is expected to be eradicated by 1995.[33]

The lever for achieving 90% has been the system of registering every birth: local doctors then notify all parents, individually, every time the infant is due for vaccination. Many countries have achieved 90% coverage for the first dose of DPT or polio only to fall behind when infants do not return for the second or third doses or for the single measles injection at the age of nine months. In China, the individual notification system means that drop-out rates have been reduced to less than 2%.

In about a third of China's counties, the system is reinforced by an 'immunization contract'. Parents pay a one-off immunization fee as soon as a child is born, and this guarantees the child all necessary injections. Thereafter, if the child contracts any vaccine-preventable disease, the family receives financial compensation.[34]

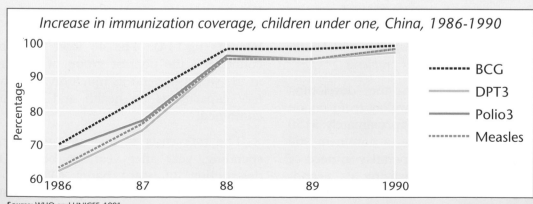

Increase in immunization coverage, children under one, China, 1986-1990

Percentage (y-axis: 60, 70, 80, 90, 100)
x-axis: 1986, 87, 88, 89, 1990

BCG
DPT3
Polio3
Measles

Source: WHO and UNICEF, 1991.

military culture has come to predominate in many developing nations in recent decades. Such a culture tends to be contemptuous of democracy, indifferent to human rights, and threatened by political, personal, and press freedoms. The total military bill in the developing world would therefore have to include the direct destruction of war, the diversion of resources from investment in people, the undermining of democracy, the growth of internal oppression, and the squandering of much of the support for development among the public of the industrialized world.

With the ending of the cold war, hopes are higher than for a generation or more that this bill might soon be reduced.

The industrialized world can do much to help. It can convert military aid into economic aid in the interests of both peace and development. It can restrict arms sales and try to prevent arms suppliers from expanding sales in the developing world to compensate for declining markets in the industrialized nations (the five permanent members of the United Nations Security Council account for 90% of the world's arms sales).[54] It can also begin to insist that debt relief, aid, and new loans, be tied to reductions in military spending, progress towards democracy, and investments in the infrastructure of health and education rather than in the infrastructure of war.

But the current disastrous levels of military spending are the one wall of the economic prison that it is within the developing world's own power to push back. And nothing less than a massive programme of demilitarization will enable many of the developing countries to fulfil their potential of the years ahead.

Demilitarization is easier said than done, not least because of the sheer importance of the military as employer (there are eight times as many soldiers in the developing world as there are doctors).[55] To ease the transition, and reduce the conflict between military and social expenditures, more thought might be given to the potential role of the armed forces in the war on poverty. It is not uncommon for the military, with their organizational capacities, their skilled personnel, their technologies, and their transport, to come to the aid of civilian populations in times of emergency or natural disaster. In the process of demobilization, it may be useful to extend that role by transfusing the skills of the military into society through the construction of infrastructure and the training of civilians in such areas as literacy, engineering, electronics, mechanics, and communications.

The conversion to development purposes of the massive investment in, and the resources and skills of, the armed forces may yet be a long way down the road. But were that journey to be taken, then many nations would find themselves able to march more quickly towards a more prosperous future and a more dignified place in an evolving new world order.

The industrialized nations

In the industrialized nations, whose annual military expenditures are approximately equal to the combined incomes of the poorest half of mankind, arms spending has fallen by approximately 3% a year for the last four years. Following the dramatic disarmament proposals announced or agreed to by four of the five permanent members of the Security Council in September 1991, even larger cuts may be expected in the years ahead. Three quarters of all the industrialized world's military expenditures of approximately $800 billion a year are currently devoted to the defence of Europe where the military landscape has been transformed. The potential for cuts in the 1990s is therefore enormous.

But what is missing is any coherent and agreed plan to link even a small part of these potentially vast savings with the desperate need of the developing world for renewed aid and investment. The allocation of even 5% of current military spending in the industrialized world would be sufficient to allow a doubling of aid budgets to the target of 0.7% of GNPs - a target that was first agreed to in the 1960s.

In particular, a proportion of military savings should be allocated to achieving the basic human goals agreed at last year's *World Summit for Children*. As a reminder, the financial cost of reaching all of those goals - including drastic reductions in malnutrition and disease and a basic education for all children - would require additional resources of approximately $20 billion a year throughout the 1990s. The developing world's proposed contribution of two thirds of that amount would require the allocation of approximately 10% of its current military expenditure. The industrialized world's one-third share would amount to 1% of its military spending.

Setting Africa free

Proposition: *That the chains of Africa's debt be struck off and that the continent be given sufficient external support to allow internal reform to succeed in regenerating the momentum of development.*

For the first time in the modern era, a subcontinent is sliding back into poverty. The number of families in sub-Saharan Africa who are unable to meet their most basic needs has doubled in a decade. Average incomes have fallen by a third. The proportion of children who are malnourished has risen. The proportion of children who are in school has fallen. This year, drought again threatens 27 million people in 14 countries. In total, 40 million Africans are now 'displaced' by military conflict or environmental disaster. And as if in a final attempt to break the spirit of a continent, almost 3 million African women are also infected with the AIDS virus and 1 million children have been born HIV positive; in the decade ahead, it is estimated that 2 million children will die and 10 million may be orphaned by the disease.

yields, mass hunger, and mass migration to the refugee camps where the problem finally becomes visible to the outside world.

As if these trials were insufficient to exercise the talents of government, Africa has also been a theatre for long-running wars and frequent *coups d'état* which have

Internal reasons

In addition to the economic losses and the conflicts caused by apartheid, the three principal internal reasons for Africa's decline are economic mismanagement, environmental degradation, and military conflict.

Autocratic governments, inefficient state corporations, large-scale corruption, unproductive investment of aid and loans, distortion of prices, markets, and exchange rates, lack of investment in food production - all these have been paid for in the falling living standards of millions of ordinary Africans. And most of the victims have had no say whatsoever in the political and economic decisions that have led to the decline in their incomes, the rising cost of their essential purchases, the absence of teachers in their schools, the bare shelves in their health centres, and the increasing malnutrition among their children.

Meanwhile, the effort to increase agricultural exports has claimed the most fertile soils and pushed desperately poor and ever growing populations onto ever more marginal lands. The result has been the overcultivation and overgrazing which have led to the tragedies of soil erosion, falling

Fig. 13 Reversing the flow

The chart shows the net financial transfers between industrialized and developing nations over the last decade. 'Net transfers' means all loans, long-term and short term, public and private, minus all interest and capital payments on previous loans.

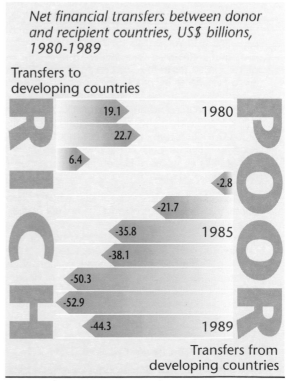

Net financial transfers between donor and recipient countries, US$ billions, 1980-1989

Transfers to developing countries

19.1 — 1980
22.7
6.4
-2.8
-21.7
-35.8 — 1985
-38.1
-50.3
-52.9
-44.3 — 1989

Transfers from developing countries

Source: World Bank, *World Debt Tables, 1990-91, Vol 1 p.126.*

Supershots: children's vaccine initiative

14

Approximately 3 million child deaths are now being prevented each year by immunization. But this represents less than a third of immunization's potential contribution to world health.

Two million children die each year because they belong to the 20% who are still not immunized with currently available vaccines. A further 5 to 6 million people die annually from diseases which could almost certainly be prevented by the development of new vaccines.[35]

The Children's Vaccine Initiative, launched by WHO, UNDP and UNICEF in September 1990,[36] aims to narrow this gap between the actual and potential contribution of immunization technology.

At present, national child immunization programmes offer vaccines against tuberculosis, diphtheria, tetanus, polio, whooping cough, and measles, with some countries also offering yellow fever and, more recently hepatitis B (panel 15). One of the challenges of the *Children's Vaccine Initiative* is to extend this range to include affordable vaccines against malaria (currently killing over 1 million African children each year), respiratory infections (3 million child deaths a year), meningitis (200,000 deaths a year), certain diarrhoeal diseases such as rotavirus (800,000 deaths a year), as well as hepatitis A, influenza B, Japanese encephalitis, dengue fever, and AIDS.[37]

Developing the vaccines is half the battle. Then come the logistical problems of ensuring widespread use. Today's vaccines against measles, polio, and tuberculosis, for example, must be kept refrigerated from point of manufacture to point of injection. Full immunization also requires four or five separate injections during the first year of life, and the drop-out rate between the first and last injection is the main barrier to higher immunization coverage.

The Children's Vaccine Initiative also aims to enlist recent breakthroughs in biotechnology to overcome some of these problems.[38]

It is now possible to incorporate several vaccines onto one carrier.[39] Vaccines can also now be packaged in microcapsules which release their contents over time, either gradually or in pulses. And it should also be possible to make most vaccines less dependent on refrigeration.

The pot of gold at the end of this research rainbow is a single-shot 'super vaccine' which could be given to children soon after birth and which would protect them against all of childhood's major infections at very low cost.

That goal may take two decades or more to achieve. But the technology for combining and time-releasing vaccines is already available. By the end of this decade, it may be possible to administer all of today's vaccines in single injection.

By the mid-1990s, time-release technology could also be helping immunization succeed in the arena of its greatest failure - the prevention of neonatal tetanus which kills an estimated 536,000 infants and an unknown number of mothers every year. The newborn child can be protected by immunizing the mother. But this requires several injections over time (or, minimally, two well-spaced injections during pregnancy) and at present, less than 50% of women are protected. A new time-release vaccine now under development offers single-shot protection and could rapidly raise coverage.[40]

Even these new technologies leave many problems unsolved - how to bring new vaccines into large-scale and inexpensive production, how to simplify production and quality control, how to speed up field trials and licencing procedures. In all of these areas, a dynamic partnership will be needed between governments and the research and development capacities of the commercial world.[36]

So far, the development of new vaccines has been driven largely by the needs and the markets of the rich nations. In the 1990s, one of the most difficult challenges will be to link that same drive to the greater needs, but narrower commercial opportunities, of the poor world.[36]

been part cause and part result of the fact that Sub-Saharan Africa as a whole has been spending two and a half times as much on its military as on its health services.

External reasons

The three principal external reasons for Africa's decline have been the use of the continent as a board for superpower games, the relative fall in world prices for its raw materials, and the unsustainable weight of its debts.

Much of Africa emerged into independence just in time to be wooed by two superpowers representing two competing ideologies. Long perceived by many African leaders as an advantage, it is clear that this superpower rivalry has in fact made a tragic contribution to the overmilitarization of the continent and to the emergence and perpetuation of the kind of military and autocratic regimes which have led so many African nations into the abyss.

Economic dependence on raw materials has been a quieter calamity. The majority of African countries have been urged to increase their earnings and pay their debts by exporting more of their primary commodities. The response has been a 25% increase in the volume of those exports during the difficult decade of the 1980s. But the steady fall in prices for Africa's raw materials, in relation to the cost of its imports, has meant that its earnings have fallen by approximately 30% in the last 10 years.[56]

Attempts to escape from this trap by diversifying exports have quickly run into the sands of tariffs and quotas by which the supposedly free-market economies of the United States, Japan, and the European Community continue to protect their own producers.

The third external factor in Africa's crisis is one which represents one of the greatest international failings of this century.

A new slavery has shackled the African continent and its name is debt. The countries of Sub-Saharan Africa, including most of the world's least developed countries, now owe a total of approximately $150 billion. Each year, Africa struggles to pay about one third of the interest which falls due; the rest is simply added to the rising mountain of debt under which the hopes of a continent lie buried.

The total inhumanity of what is now happening is reflected in the single fact that even the small proportion of the interest which Africa does manage to pay is absorbing a quarter of all its export earnings[57] and costing the continent, each year, *more than its total spending on the health and education of its people* (fig. 8).

To date, the results of the Paris Club debt re-scheduling exercise and the Toronto Agreement are entirely inadequate.[58] Excluding Egypt, the total of African debt written off is approximately $7 billion out of the $280 billion owed. The consequent reduction in interest payments amounts to about $0.2 billion out of the $32 billion falling due and the $12 billion actually being paid each year.[59] Between now and the end of the century, even the full implementation of the Toronto Terms is unlikely to reduce Africa's outflow of interest payments by any more than 5%.[60]

The most recent debt reduction proposals, the Trinidad Terms, still do not represent even the beginnings of a solution commensurate with the scale of the problem. The most generous notion on the table (and it is a long way from being agreed) would reduce Africa's total indebtedness by between $20 and $30 billion. That would mean a reduction of perhaps $3 or $4 billion a year in the interest due, but very little reduction in the actual interest paid. The greatest hope on the present horizon, therefore, is that Africa will be slightly better off on paper while in practice the financial haemorrhage will continue unstaunched.

In one of the most recent and comprehensive analyses of Africa's debt and the efforts to reduce it, the economist Percy Mistry comes to the *"inescapable conclusion that these efforts have not been even remotely effective in achieving the objective of relieving [debt] burdens sufficiently for African countries to have a reasonable chance of success in achieving structural adjustment, recovery, or growth, in the foreseeable future, unless previous desultory approaches to debt relief are abandoned in favour of more dramatic but absolutely necessary and long overdue action."*[61]

Moral hazard

If a continent is not to be left behind as the rest of the world struggles towards a new peace and a new prosperity, then extraordinary measures are now called for.

Ten years of prevarication over this problem has already damaged not only the Africa of today but the Africa of tomorrow. While more than $10 billion a year is being sluiced out of that desperately poor continent in interest repayments, tens of millions of children are losing their one opportunity to grow normally, to go to school and become literate, and to acquire the skills necessary for their own and their countries' development in the years to come.

It is claimed that the industrialized world can do no better at the present time. Yet ways have been found to halve Egypt's $40 billion debt following the Gulf war and to make a similar concession to Poland following the liberation of Eastern Europe.

It is claimed that a more drastic reduction in Africa's debts would constitute a 'moral hazard' by rewarding those who do not pay their debts. But the real moral hazard is surely to the soul of a world which is prepared to condemn a continent to continued poverty, and a generation of its children to malnutrition, for the sake of collecting interest on moneys which were often irresponsibly lent and most of which cannot possibly be repaid.

It is also claimed that debt forgiveness would help to sustain failed economic policies. But the majority of African countries have already begun implementing basic economic reforms.

Events in Eastern Europe and the Soviet Union, coinciding with a clearly marked 'end of the road' for the kinds of political and economic systems that have prevailed across so much of Africa in recent decades, have had a profound effect on the continent. Most countries have now begun to take the first steps towards democracy, pluralism, and market-oriented economic reform. The prospects for renewed economic growth and social progress should be

Fig. 14 War versus welfare

The graph contrasts the rise in military expenditure, (dashed lines), with the decline in welfare expenditures, (solid lines), in some of the poorest African countries over the last two decades.

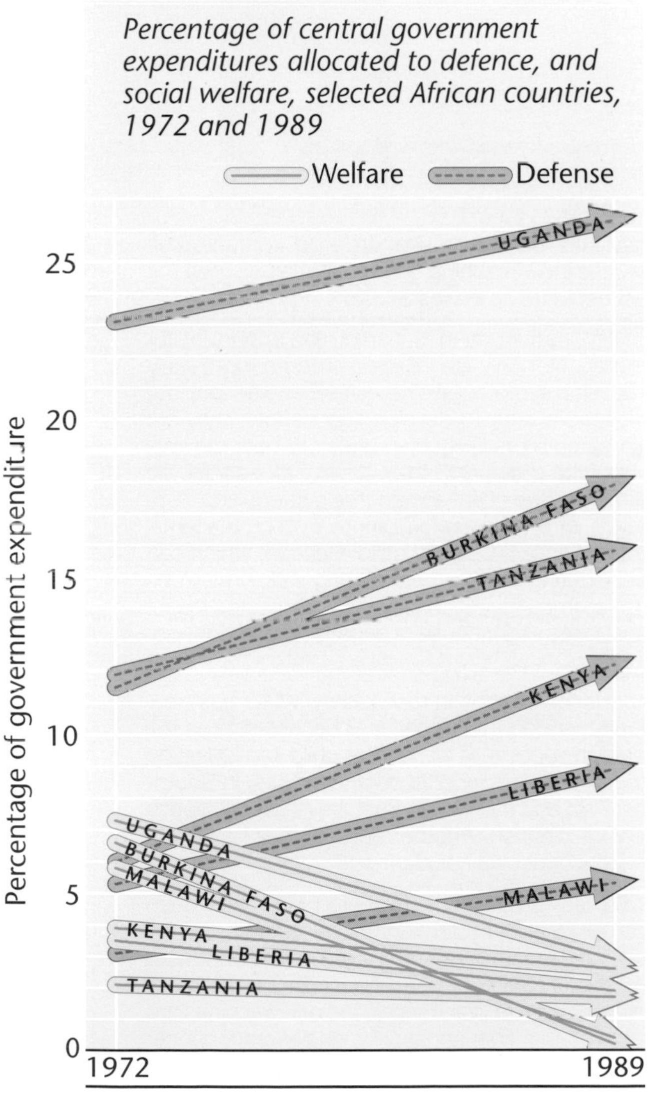

Percentage of central government expenditures allocated to defence, and social welfare, selected African countries, 1972 and 1989

Welfare expenditures include housing and slum clearance; community development; payments to the sick, the disabled, the elderly and the unemployed; family, maternity and child allowances; welfare services for the elderly, the disabled, and children; pollution abatement, water supply and sanitation.

Source: World Bank, *World development Reports*, 1989, 1990, 1991.

stronger in the 1990s than at any time in the last two decades.

With these changes, the hopes of a continent have again been awakened. If those hopes cannot manage to escape from under the weight of past debts, then the result will again be the despair and frustration which are the natural habitat of dictators and demagogues. If Africa is to evolve towards a new internal order, and to find a dignified place in the new world order, then the present opportunity must not be lost. The ways and means should now be found to absolve Africa of the great majority of its bi-lateral and international debts.

The democratic choice

The new spirit moving in Africa today was summed up in a recent address to Africa's heads of state delivered by the Nigerian President, Ibrahim Babangida:[62]

"There is no lasting substitute for a profound and painful commitment at home to reconstitute our societies, to reform our political systems, and to restructure our economies ...

"Sovereignty was indeed wrested from us as a people. That fact is rooted in our history. Equally undeniable, however, is the fact that with the act of recovering that sovereignty ... African leadership in general did not give much thought to the logic and justice of reinvesting that sovereignty in its peoples.

"Democracy is not only an attractive option but a rational and inevitable one. This is one act of our internal reparations which leadership on this continent can no longer evade.

Hepatitis B:
the seventh vaccine

15

The global immunization system, built during the 1980s to deliver vaccines against tuberculosis, diphtheria, polio, tetanus, whooping cough, and measles, could be used in the 1990s to control hepatitis B - one of the world's greatest health scourges.

Hepatitis B kills more people every day than AIDS kills in a year. It is responsible for about 80% of all liver cancers and more cases of liver cirrhosis (60 million worldwide) than alcohol.[41]

One person in six in the world has been infected with the disease, and approximately 300 million are chronic carriers[2]. The virus is incurable (although the body may rid itself of the infection) and is transmitted by a range of body fluids, mainly through sexual activity but also via contact with contaminated blood, by placental transmission from mother to unborn child, and by skin lesions, which are the main means of transmission in children.

About a third of all those infected with hepatitis B develop chronic symptoms. After the acute phase has passed, about 6% to 10% of these victims become carriers of the disease.[42] Although not necessarily showing any symptoms, despite progressive and possibly fatal liver damage, they join the 300 million pool of chronic carriers who spread the virus and perpetuate it from one generation to the next.

Immunization against hepatitis B has been available for some time. But because the vaccine was derived from blood given by a carrier of the virus, it could only be produced in small quantities. The cost, until the late 1980s, was $110 per three-shot course.[43] Now, genetic engineering has made it possible to produce larger quantities of the vaccine at a cost of $2.80 per course. If the new vaccine

goes into worldwide use via child immunization services (now reaching 80% of all infants), then the cost could fall as low as $1.50.[42]

HBV immunization is particularly important for children. Not only are infected children more likely to develop symptomatic hepatitis B and almost four times more likely to develop liver cancer, they are also much more likely than adults to become carriers of the disease. One quarter of those infected before the age of seven become carriers (and 70% to 90% of those infected before birth by placental transmission).[44] Child-to-child infection, which can occur during play or bed-sharing via skin lesions such as impetigo, scabies, cuts and infected insect bites, is the major cause of hepatitis B in childhood.

In view of the falling cost of the vaccine and the importance of early immunization, WHO has now recommended that hepatitis B be included as the 'seventh vaccine' in all national child immunization programmes. So far, 22 countries, mainly in South-East Asia and the Middle East, have begun routine HBV vaccination. Another 50 countries have pilot projects under way or planned.[43]

So far, genetically engineered HBV has been used on more than 50 million people worldwide and has been found to be one of the safest and most effective of all vaccines. And because hepatitis B is a major cause of liver cancer, the new vaccines are in effect the first genetically engineered cancer immunization.

It is therefore technically feasible to eradicate hepatitis B. The worldwide cost is likely to be upwards of $100 million a year. With the expensive part - the delivery system - already in place, and with so much human health at stake, it would surely be unthinkable if the resources were not found.

"Today, the clamour for democratization and party pluralism is on the ascendancy in Africa. As leaders, we must accept and comply with the wishes of those whom we represent. No amount of force can forever stifle the right of the governed to decide, at periodic, free and fair elections, the fate of any government.

"The ravages of civil unrest right across our continent, the consequent retardation of creativity for our human potential, the intolerable flow of millions of our humanity turned refugees from their own lands ... constitute a permanent rebuke to our political judgement and will ... The only viable alternative is a sincere embrace of the democratic option. Let us take the resolve now, and commit ourselves to the dismantling of all apparatus of unrepresentative power, setting a date before the end of this century for its achievement."

President Babangida's call for *'internal reparations'* is the counterpart to his call *"for Africa as a whole to fight in all possible ways the just battle for international reparations against the centuries of humiliation and exploitation to which it has been subjected ... For Africa*, he concluded, *"that should be the proper starting point of a meaningful New World Order."*

In response to such calls and to the new spirit evident in Africa, and as a gesture of reparation for exploitation in the past and preparation for a new partnership in the future, Africa should now be absolved of most of its debts.

The cost to the industrialized world would be by no means crippling. Sub-Saharan Africa's total debt amounts to only about 12% of the debts of the developing world as a whole. But for Africa, the sheer weight of the ball and chain of debt and interest repayments now means that there is no realistic possibility of forward movement until its financial shackles are struck off.

A conference for the African child

While attempting to tackle these fundamental problems, most African nations are also preparing National Programmes of Action with the specific aim of meeting the goals agreed at the *World Summit for Children.* The process of funding progress towards such goals as halving malnutrition, reducing the impact of the most common diseases, bringing clean water to all communities, and ensuring that all children have access to basic education, will be most difficult of all in the Sub-Saharan African region. Late in 1992, the Organization of African Unity intends to call an international conference to draw attention to the action which Africa is already taking to try to reach those goals and to seek the support of the international community in sustaining that action in the 1990s. Africa will need to find at least $1.5 billion a year from its own resources, via a re-ordering of its internal priorities, but will need about the same amount in international aid if progress towards these goals for its children - and its future - is to be maintained. The response will be one of the first opportunities for the world to reach out the hand of a new partnership with Africa, and to signal that Africa, too, has a place in a new world order.

Facts for Life: messages for millions

16

There is today a body of basic child health information - about safe motherhood, birth spacing, breastfeeding, child growth, illness prevention, oral rehydration, immunization, and AIDS - which most parents could act on and which could protect millions of children. It is therefore information which all families now have a right to know.

To help make that right into a reality, *Facts for Life* was published in 1989 by UNICEF, UNESCO and WHO in partnership with 100 of the world's best-known organizations working for children.[45] The booklet presents, as a series of 55 simple messages, today's scientific consensus on practical, low-cost, family-based ways of protecting children's lives and health.

There has been a worldwide response to *Facts for Life*. Over 3.5 million copies have been published in 120 languages and 90 countries.

Facts for Life is now part of the school curriculum and/or literacy programmes in Algeria, Bangladesh, Bhutan, Burundi, Cape Verde, Djibouti, Ecuador, Egypt, Ethiopia, Iran, Jamaica, Kenya, Madagascar, Mauritius, Mexico, Nepal, Nicaragua, Pakistan, Philippines, Rwanda, Sierra Leone, Sudan, Swaziland, Tanzania, Thailand, Turkey, Viet Nam and Yemen.

The health services of most countries have begun using *Facts for Life*. In Turkey, 1 million leaflets and tens of thousands of Facts for Life posters are helping midwives, nurses and doctors to reach families. In Jamaica, the publication has been adapted for all health centres. In Ecuador, nurses and medical students use *Facts for Life* for compulsory community service. In Sierra Leone, the health service is training 1,400 teachers, health workers and agricultural extension workers to use *Facts for Life*. In Viet Nam, 25,000 *Facts for Life* communicators are being trained by the Ministry of Health.

In almost every country, the mass media have responded with regular TV and radio spots, serializations of the booklet, quizzes and competitions, and the inclusion of messages in hundreds of soap operas and popular radio programmes.

Political leaders have also helped. The Thai version was launched by the Deputy Prime Minister, who said "*Facts for Life is a practical gift of lasting wisdom to all parents*". President Corazon Aquino of the Philippines ordered it to be translated into all 10 major dialects - five have been completed so far. President Joaquim Chissano of Mozambique launched the national version and called on all the nation's communicators to promote its messages. In Viet Nam, the Vice-President of the Council of Ministers announced, "*The Government of Viet Nam, the people of Viet Nam, undertake the challenge of communicating Facts for Life for the happiness of all mothers and children*".

In China, 1 million copies have been published in 12 languages.

In Brazil, a major supermarket chain has put *Facts For Life* messages on 120 million plastic bags. In Kenya, 10 million matchboxes carry the messages. In Turkey, they have appeared on 2 million milk cartons.

In Iran, *Facts for Life* has been adapted for the National Literacy Campaign, reaching 2 million people - mainly women.

In Mexico, 380,000 copies of the national version have been distributed out of a planned-for 1 million.

In Myanmar, 200,000 copies of the national version have been produced for schools, health centres, water and sanitation workers, and religious organizations.

In Nigeria, 300,000 copies have been produced in four major languages for schools, nursing colleges and religious leaders.

In Sri Lanka, the Broadcasting Corporation has organized a national *Facts for Life* quiz for 10,000 schools.

In Turkey, *Facts for Life* is reaching all schoolchildren via the training of 250,000 teachers and 1,500 school inspectors. Over a million *Facts for Life* leaflets have been used by 65,000 imams in Friday sermons.

The apartheid of gender

Proposition: *That a new world order should oppose the apartheid of gender as vigorously as the apartheid of race.*

The one constant of the developing world, whether in Africa, Asia, or Latin America, whether in city slum or rural villages, whether in the depths of economic despair or at the height of economic activity, is that women will be working from first light until after dark to meet their families' many needs.

It is a commonplace that the developing world's women bear and care for its children, fetch and carry its fuel and water, cook its meals and shop for its needs, wash its clothes and clean its homes, and look after its old and its ill. It is less widely known that women also grow and market most of the developing world's food, earn an increasing proportion of its income, and work, on average, twice as many hours a day as men.[63]

In return for this disproportionate contribution, the women of the developing world are generally rewarded with less food, less health care, less education, less training, less leisure, less income, less rights and less protection.

So heavy is this weight of discrimination that it even sways the survival chances of the girl child. All other things being equal, girl children have a better natural chance of surviving the early, vulnerable years. But all other things are not equal. In several countries of South Asia, fewer girls survive than boys.[64] And in this gap between natural and actual survival rates, discrimination can be measured. In Bangladesh, India, and Pakistan it adds up to more than a million deaths every year. In other words, a million girls die each year because they are born female.

If a new world order is to attempt to put right the most glaring failings of the old, then this issue of discrimination against women cannot be omitted from the agenda. Yet the severity and scale of this injustice has not yet been widely accepted. It is, for example, an injustice on a far greater scale than the apartheid system that has aroused the fervent and sustained opposition of the international community in recent decades. The abhorrence with which the whole world has rightly regarded apartheid is an abhorrence born of the simple moral proposition that a peoples' rights and opportunities - where they can live, what education and health care they will receive, what job they can do, what income they can earn, what legal standing they will have - should not depend on whether they are born black or white. Yet it seems that the world is prepared to accept, with none of the depth and breadth of opposition that has been seen during the apartheid years, that all of these things can depend upon the accident of being born male or female.

There is little exaggeration in this comparison. In the developing world today, many more boys become literate than girls. In some countries, twice as many boys as girls are brought to health centres for treatment. Employment rights, social security rights, legal rights, property rights, and even civil and political liberties are all likely to depend upon the one, cruel chromosome.

The practical costs of this bias are the reduced effectiveness of almost every other aspect of the development process.

But to discriminate against girls in the matter of educational opportunity is perhaps the biggest practical mistake of all. Over many years and in many countries, the education of women has been shown to be associated with the confidence to adopt new ways, the propensity to make greater use of social services, the ability to earn higher incomes, the improvement of child care and nutrition, the reduction of child deaths, the acceptance of family planning, the reduction of average family size, and the literacy of the succeeding generation.[65]

The education of girls is therefore another of those extraordinary points of leverage which could advance the world towards many of the other goals discussed in this report. It is also a principal means of righting one of the most evident of all wrongs in the existing world order.

Planning births

Proposition: *That the responsible planning of births is one of the most effective and least expensive ways of improving the quality of life on earth - both now and in the future - and that one of the greatest mistakes of our times is the failure to realise that potential.*

Family planning could bring more benefits to more people at less cost than any other single 'technology' now available to the human race. But it is not appreciated widely enough that this would still be true even if there were no such thing as a population problem.

In part, an awareness of the full range of the benefits available from the responsible planning of families has been hidden from the public view by the clouds of controversy which have long hung over this issue. But such is the range of methods now available, and such the experience that has been gained in recent years, that family planning can now be promoted and practised in ways which are sensitive to the religious and cultural contours of almost all societies. The benefits of family planning need be denied to no one.

Those benefits may be briefly summarized:

First, family planning could save the lives of perhaps one quarter to one third of the 500,000 women who now die every year from causes related to pregnancy and giving birth.[66] It could also prevent unknown millions of disabilities - many of them painful, permanent, embarrassing, and secret - which are the common consequence of high-risk and often unwanted births.[67]

Second, family planning could prevent many if not most of the more than 50,000 illegal abortions which are now performed on women *every single day* and which result in the deaths of 150,000 young women every year.[68]

Third, family planning can drastically improve the quality of women's lives - in both short and long term - by reducing the physical and mental burdens of having too many children too close together, or at too early or too late an age. It can increase the time available for women's education, for vocational training, for earning incomes, for improving child care, for community activities, for personal development, and for the rest and leisure which is virtually unknown to millions of women in the developing world today.

Fourth, family planning could save the lives of several million children each year. Family planning would prevent, predominantly, those births which are known to be 'high risk' - the births which are within two years of a previous birth, or to mothers who are under 18 or over 35 or who already have three or four or more children.[69] Because the great majority of child deaths are associated with these risk factors, the well-informed timing and spacing of births would result in a far more than proportionate reduction in child deaths.

Fifth, family planning can significantly improve the nutritional health of children throughout the developing world. Fewer and more widely spaced births allow mothers more time for breastfeeding and weaning, and helps to prevent the low birth weights which are strongly associated with malnutrition throughout the earliest years of life.[70]

Sixth, family planning improves the quality of life for children. The quality of child care - including play and stimulation as well as health and education - inevitably rises as parents are able to invest more of their time, energy, and money in bringing up a smaller number of children.

For all of these reasons, a renewed effort to put family planning at the disposal of all would advance not one but many of the basic human goals for the year 2000 which were agreed at the *World Summit for Children.*

These benefits alone would be sufficient to justify the claim of 'family planning for all' to a special priority in a new world order. But it would, of course, also help to resolve one of the other great problems on the human agenda - the problem of rapid population growth.

Approximately one pregnancy in three in the developing world this year will be not only unplanned but unwanted.[71] There is therefore a vast unmet demand for the knowledge and the means of family planning.

Evidence from the *World Fertility Survey* suggests that if all women in the developing world who do not wish to become pregnant were empowered to exercise that choice then the rate of population growth would fall by approximately 30%.[72] By the year 2025, that fall would translate into 1.3 billion fewer people - roughly the equivalent of the population of China today.[73]

Even this long list of benefits does not capture the potential contribution of family planning to the improvement of the human condition. For it fails to record the synergisms which mean that the total benefit would be very much greater than the sum of the parts. Within the sphere of human health, family planning reinforces, and is reinforced by, progress towards almost all other improvements in the health and well-being of both mothers and children. The timing and spacing of births, for example, leads to improved health and nutrition, which in turn leads to fewer deaths; this helps to build confidence in family planning and the tendency towards more widely spaced births. An upward spiral is therefore set in motion. But there is also a wider circle of synergisms of which birth spacing and family planning stand close to the centre. Fewer and more widely spaced births improves the quality of women's lives, of child care, of family life, of education; all of these contribute to social and economic progress, which in turn contributes to the wider acceptance of family planning.

The permutations of such synergisms are almost limitless. And uniting them all is the fact that family planning gives people more control over their own lives and enables them to bring about other improvements in almost every aspect of those lives. It means better health and wider opportunities for hundreds of millions of women. It means fewer deaths and better physical and mental growth for hundreds of millions of children. It means improved standards of living and less strain on social services. It also means slower population growth and an easing of environmental pressures in the future. The costs, in relation to these benefits, are almost absurdly small.

When so much stands to be achieved by the meeting of an existing demand and at so low a cost, it seems reasonable to propose, for the agenda of any new world order, that an effort now be made, on an entirely new scale, to put the knowledge and the means of family planning at the disposal of every couple of child-bearing age before the end of this present century. □

Year 2000 goals

The following is the full list of goals, to be attained by the year 2000, which were adopted by the *World Summit for Children* on September 30 1990. After widespread consultation among governments and the agencies of the United Nations, these targets were considered to be feasible and financially affordable over the course of the decade ahead.

Overall goals 1990-2000

○ A one-third reduction in under-five death rates (or a reduction to below 70 per 1,000 live births whichever is less).

○ A halving of maternal mortality rates.

○ A halving of severe and moderate malnutrition among the world's under-fives.

○ Safe water and sanitation for all families.

○ Basic education for all children and completion of primary education by at least 80%.

○ A halving of the adult illiteracy rate and the achievement of equal educational opportunity for males and females.

○ Protection for the many millions of children in especially difficult circumstances and the acceptance and observance, in all countries, of the recently adopted Convention on the Rights of the Child. In particular, the 1990s should see rapidly growing acceptance of the idea of special protection for children in time of war.

Protection for girls and women

○ Family planning education and services to be made available to all couples to empower them to prevent unwanted pregnancies and births which are 'too many and too close' and to women who are 'too young or too old'.

○ All women to have access to pre-natal care, a trained attendant during childbirth and referral for high-risk pregnancies and obstetric emergencies.

○ Universal recognition of the special health and nutritional needs of females during early childhood, adolescence, pregnancy and lactation.

Nutrition

○ A reduction in the incidence of low birth weight (less than 2.5 kg.) to less than 10%.

○ A one-third reduction in iron deficiency anaemia among women.

○ Virtual elimination of vitamin A deficiency and iodine deficiency disorders.

○ All families to know the importance of supporting women in the task of exclusive breastfeeding for the first four to six months of a child's life and of meeting the special feeding needs of a young child through the vulnerable years.

○ Growth monitoring and promotion to be institutionalized in all countries.

○ Dissemination of knowledge to enable all families to ensure household food security.

Child health

○ The eradication of polio.

○ The elimination of neonatal tetanus (by 1995).

○ A 90% reduction in measles cases and a 95% reduction in measles deaths, compared to pre-immunization levels.

○ Achievement and maintenance of at least 90% immunization coverage of one-year-old children and universal tetanus immunization for women in the child-bearing years.

○ A halving of child deaths caused by diarrhoea and a 25% reduction in the incidence of diarrhoeal diseases.

○ A one-third reduction in child deaths caused by acute respiratory infections.

○ The elimination of guinea worm disease.

Education

○ In addition to the expansion of primary school education and its equivalents, today's essential knowledge and life skills could be put at the disposal of all families by mobilizing today's vastly increased communications capacity.

References

1 World Health Organization, 'Causes of Deaths Among Children Under 5 Years, Developing Countries, 1985 and 1990 Estimates', WHO, Geneva, September 1991

2 World Health Organization, 'Expanded Programme of Immunization, Global Overview', EPI Gobal Advisory Group, WHO, Geneva, 1991, EPI/GAC/91 WP.1, p. 2

3 United Nations Children's Fund, 'World Declaration on the survival, protection and development of children' and 'Plan of action for implementing the world declaration on the survival, protection and development of children in the 1990s', *The State of the World's Children* 1991, UNICEF, New York 1990

4 Grant, James P., *The State of the World's Children* 1991, Oxford University Press, 1990

5 United Nations Children's Fund, *Children and Development in the 1990s: a UNICEF sourcebook,* UNICEF, New York, 1990

6 Sivard, Ruth Leger, *World Military and Social Expenditures,* 1990

7 World Health Organization, EPI for the 1990s, First Phase: 1991-1994, 'Targeting Diseases to Strengthen National Immunization Programmes', an information document, WHO, Expanded Programme on Immunization, Geneva, WHO/EPI/GEN/91.4

8 Rosero-Bixby, Luis, 'Infant Mortality in Costa Rica: Explaining the Recent Decline', Studies in Family Planning, Vol. 17, No. 2, pp. 57-65, March/April 1986

   Khan, M.U. and Ahmad, K., 'Withdrawal of Food During Diarrhoea: Major Mechanism of Malnutrition Following Diarrhoea in Bangladesh Children', Journal of Tropical Paediatrics, Vol. 32, pp. 57-61, April 1986, Oxford University Press

   Population Immunization Program, 'Immunizing the World's Children', Population Reports, Vol. xiv, No. 1, Johns Hopkins University, Baltimore

   Payne, Philip, 'Appropriate Indicators for Project Design and Evaluation', *Food Aid and the Well-Being of Children in the Developing World,* pp. 109-141, United Nations Children's Fund, World Food Programme, 1986

   World Health Organization, 'Workshop on appropriate uses of anthropometric indices in children' (draft report), SCN secretariat, WHO, Geneva, ACC/SCN, 1989

9 World Health Organization, Programme for Control of Diarrhoeal Diseases, 'Interim Programme Report', CDD/91.36, p. 17, WHO, Geneva, 1990

10 Rotary International, 'Polioplus Program Statement of Purpose', *Report on Operations 1989-90,* June 1990

11 United Nations Children's Fund, 'World Declaration on the survival, protection and development of children' and 'Plan of action for implementing the world declaration on the survival, protection and development of children in the 1990s', *The State of the World's Children 1991,* UNICEF, New York 1990

12 United Nations Children's Fund, *Children on the Front Line. The impact of apartheid, destabilization and warfare on children in southern and South Africa,* UNICEF, New York, 1989 update

13 UNICEF's first special study on this topic, *The Impact of World Recession on Children,* was published in 1984. A more detailed follow-up study, *Adjustment with a Human Face,* edited by Giovanni Andrea Cornia, Richard Jolly and Frances Stewart, has been published in English in two volumes by Oxford University Press

14 Albanez, T., Bustelo, E., Cornia, G.A. and Jespersen, E., *Economic Decline and Child Survival: The Plight of Latin America in the Eighties,* UNICEF, International Child Development Centre, Florence, Innocenti Occasional Papers No. 1, March 1989

15 Berstecher, D. and Carr-Hill, R., 'Primary Education and Economic Recession in the Developing World Since 1980', a special study for the World Conference on Education for All, Thailand, 5-9 March 1990, UNESCO, New York, 1990

16 'Report of the International Study Team: Conditions in Iraq, October 1991', reported in *The Independent,* London, 20 September 1991

17 Cornia G.A. and Sipos, S., *Children and the Transition to the Market Economy: Safety Nets and Social Policies in Central and Eastern Europe,* UNICEF, International Child Development Centre, Florence, 1991

18 Internal UNICEF memorandum in connection with the UNICEF mission to Albania, July 1991

19 Cornia, G.A., *Child Poverty and Deprivation in Industrialized Countries: Recent Trends and Policy Options,* UNICEF, International Child Development Centre, Florence, Innocenti Occasional Papers No. 2, March 1990

   Bradshaw, Jonathan, *Child Poverty and Deprivation in the UK,* UNICEF, International Child Development Centre, Florence, Innocenti Occasional Papers No. 8, October 1990

   Danziger, S. and Stern, J., *The Causes and Consequences of Child Poverty in the United States,* UNICEF, International Child Development Centre, Florence, Innocenti Occasional Papers No. 10, November 1990

20 Johnson, C.M., Miranda, L., Sherman, A. and Weill, J.D., *Child Poverty in America,* Children's Defense Fund, 122 C Street, N.W., Washington, D.C. 20001

21 Griffin, K. and Knight, J., 'Human Development: The Case for Renewed Emphasis', *Human Development in the 1980s and Beyond,* p. 22, United Nations, 1989

   'Unequal gains', *The Economist,* p. 25, 10 August 1991

22 Raczynski, D., 'Política social, probreza y grupos vulnerables: La infancia en Chile', in *Adjustment with a Human Face, Volume I: Protecting the Vulnerable and Promoting Growth,* Cornia, G.A., Jolly, R. and Stewart, F. (eds.), pp. 69-118, Oxford University Press, 1987

23 Mohs, Dr. Edgar, *General Theory of Paradigms in Health,* Hospital Nacional de Niños, San José, Costa Rica

24 Lloyd, C.B. and Ivanov, S., 'The Effects of Improved Child Survival on Family Planning Practice and Fertility' *Studies in Family Planning,* Vol. 19, No. 3, pp. 141-161, May/June 1988

   United Nations, 'Family Building by Fate or Design', A Study of Relationships between Child Survival and Fertility', ST/ESA/SER.R/74, United Nations, Department of International Economic and Social Affairs, New York

25 South Commission, *The Challenge to the South, overview and summary of the South Commission Report*

26 Wade, Robert, Governing the Market: *Economic Theory and the Role of Government in East Asian Industrialization,* Princeton University Press, 1991

27 See, for example, Lewis, J.P. and Kallab, V., *Development Strategies Reconsidered,* Overseas Development Council, Washington D.C.

28 South Commission, op. cit., p. 15

29 World Bank, *World Development Report 1991,* p. 43, World Bank, Washington, D.C., 1991

30 Jamison, D., and Lau, L., *Farmer Education and Farm Efficiency,* Johns Hopkins University Press, Baltimore, 1982

31 See Scrimshaw 1986 and McGuire and Austin 1987 in Cornia, G.A., 'Investing in Human Resources: Health Nutrition and Development for the 1990s', *Human Development in the 1980s and Beyond,* p. 179, United Nations, 1989. Also, World Bank, op. cit., p. 43

32 World Health Organization, *International Water and Sanitation Decade 1981-1990:* Decade Assessment, WHO, Geneva, 1990

33 Cornia, op. cit., pp. 175-176

34 World Bank, op. cit., p. 66

35 Interview with Dr. Hiroshi Nakajima, Director-General, World Health Organization, in *Development Forum,* Vol. xviii, No. 2, March-April, 1990, United Nations Department of Public Information, New York

36 United Nations Development Programme, *Human Development Report 1991,* p. 51, UNDP, New York

37 Psacharopoulos, George, 'Critical Issues in Education: A World Agenda', a discussion paper, World Bank, Education and Training Department, Washington, D.C., 1987

38 Oxenham, J. and de Jong, J., 'Improving the quality of education in developing countries', *Human Development in the 1990s and Beyond,* p. 121, United Nations, Department of International Economic and Social Affairs, New York, 1989

39 World Bank, op. cit., pp. 64-66

40 United Nations Children's Fund, *The BRAC non-formal primary education programme in Bangladesh,* UNICEF, New York, 1989

41 Address by Barber B. Conable, President, World Bank, to the Board of Governors of the World Bank Group, Berlin, 27 September 1988

42 See, for example, McGinn, Noel F., Snodgrass, R., Kim, Yung Bong, and Kim, Shin-Bok, *Education and Development in Korea,* chapter 5, p. 185, Harvard University Press, 1980

43 Fredriksen, Birger, 'Increasing Foreign Aid for Primary Education: The Challenge to Donors', PHREE/90/30, World Bank, Education and Employment Division, Population and Human Resources Department, Washington, D.C., 1990

44 'Australians' attitudes to overseas aid and development', *Australian International Development Issues,* No. 8, Report from the National Social Science Survey, Institute of Advanced Studies, Australian National University

45 Cornia, G.A., 'Global Socioeconomic Changes and Child Welfare: What will the 21st Century bring us?' in Chan, Betty Po-King, (ed.), *Early Childhood Toward the 21st Century: A Worldwide Perspective,* Yew Chung Education Publishing Company, Hong Kong, 1990

46 World Bank, *Annual Report 1991,* World Bank, Washington, D.C.

47 'A Prospect of Growth' *The Economist,* p. 15, 13 July 1991

48 World Bank, op. cit., p. 11

49 Speech given by Michel Camdessus, Managing Director of the International Monetary Fund to the meeting of World Trade Ministers, Brussels, December 1990

50 'Reconstructing Kuwait and Iraq: Picking up the Pieces', *The Economist,* p. 28, 2 March 1991

Fracassi, F. and Petrucci, P. 'Il Costo Dello Guerra', *Avvenimenti,* pp. 10-11, 20 March 1991

51 World Bank, op. cit., pp. 10-11

52 Sivard, op. cit.

53 Stockholm International Peace Research Institute, *SIPRI Yearbook 1990: World Armaments and Disarmament,* SIPRI, Oxford University Press, 1990

54 ibid.

55 Sivard, op. cit.

56 Faini, R., de Melo, J., Senhadj-Semlali, A. and Stanton, J. 'Growth-oriented Adjustment Programs: A statistical Analysis', *Development Studies Working Paper,* No. 14, Torino and Oxford, Centro Studi Luca d'Agliano-Queen Elizabeth House

Mistry, Percy S., Senior Fellow, International Finance, Queen Elizabeth House, University of Oxford, 'African Debt Revisited: Procrastination or Progress?', paper prepared for the North-South Roundtable on African Debt Relief, Recovery and Democracy, Abidjan, 8-9 July 1991

57 Address by General Ibrahim Badamasi Babangida, President, Federal Republic of Nigeria at the 27th ordinary assembly of OAU heads of State and Government, Abuja, Nigeria, 3 June 1991

58 Helleiner, G.K., *The IMF, the World Bank, and Africa's adjustment and external debt problems: an unofficial view,* University of Toronto, Department of Economics, 1991

59 ibid.

Mistry, op. cit.

60 Helleiner, op. cit.

61 Mistry, op. cit.

62 Address by General Babangida, op. cit.

63 45th World Health Assembly, provisional agenda item 20, 'Women, Health and Development', progress report by the Director General, A44/15, p. 4, 4 April 1991

64 World Bank, op. cit., Table 32, 'Women in Development'. p. 266

65 World Bank, op. cit., p. 49

66 45th World Health Assembly, op. cit.

Rosenfield, A. and Maine, D., 'Maternal Mortality - A Neglected Tragedy', *The Lancet,* 13 July 1985

Fauveau, V., Koenig, M.A., Woyjtyniak, B. and Chakraborty, J., 'Impact of a family planning and health service programme on adult female mortality', *Health Policy and Planning,* 3(4), pp. 271-279

Winikoff B., Carignan, C., Bernardik, E. and Semeraro, P., 'Medical services to save mothers' lives: Feasible approaches to reducing maternal mortality', background paper for Safe Motherhood International Conference, World Bank, Nairobi, 10-13 February 1987

67 World Health Organization, 'The Status of Women, Maternal Health and Maternal Mortality', paper presented at the Safe Motherhood International Conference, Nairobi, 10-13 February 1987

68 Wallace, H.M., and Giri, K., *Health Care of Women and Children in Developing Countries,* pp. 199-200, Third Party Publishing, California

World Health Organization, *Safe Motherhood,* Issue 5, p. 8, March-June 1991, WHO, Geneva

69 Population Immunization Program, 'Healthier Mothers and Children through Family Planning', *Population Reports,* Vol. xii, No. 3, Johns Hopkins University, Baltimore

Trussell, J. and Pebley, A.R., 'The Potential Impact of Changes in Fertility and Infant, Child, and Maternal Mortality', *Studies in Family Planning,* Vol. 15, No. 6, pp. 267-280, Nov./Dec. 1988

70 Rohde, Jon, *Strategies for Reducing Perinatal Mortality: A View from the Community,* UNICEF, New Delhi, 1991

Oduntan, S. Olu, 'Low Birth Weight', in Wallace and Giri, op. cit., pp. 292-300

71 Wallace and Giri, op. cit., pp. 196-197

Cleland, J. and Hobcraft, J., (eds.), *Reproductive Change in Developing Countries, Insights from the World Fertility Survey,* p. 128, Oxford University Press, 1985

Lightbourne, R. and Singh, S. with Green, C.P., 'The World Fertility Survey: Charting Global Childbearing', *Population Bulletin,* Vol. 37, No. 1, Population Reference Bureau, Washington, D.C., 1982

72 Cornia, G.A., 'Investing in human resources: health, nutrition and development for the 1990s', *Human development in the 1980s and beyond,* pp. 175-176, United Nations, 1989

73 Hill, Ken, Johns Hopkins University, School of Hygiene and Public Health, using the United Nations and World Bank Population Projection Models

Panel references

1   For the full text of the 'Summit Declaration and Plan of Action' (including the year 2000 goals), plus the text of the 'Convention on the Rights of the Child', please see *The State of the World's Children 1991,* available from UNICEF offices or from Oxford University Press

2   WHO, Geneva, August, 1991

3   'Universal Child Immunization 1990', progress report to the Economic and Social Council of the United Nations, UNICEF, New York, 20 March 1991

4   Division of Immunization, Centers for Disease Control, U.S. Public Health Service, 1991

5   Kim-Farley, Dr. Robert, Director, Expanded Programme on Immunization, WHO, Geneva

6   UNICEF, Nairobi, 1991

7   World Health Organization, 'Expanded Programme of Immunization, Global Overview', EPI Gobal Advisory Group, WHO, Geneva, 1991, EPI/Gcn/91.3

8   Henderson, Dr. R.H., Kim-Farley, Dr. R. and Chan, C., 'Reaping the Benefits: Disease Control through Immunization in the 1990s', WHO, Geneva, 1990

9   Rohde, Dr. Jon, 'Measuring Universal Child Immunization', UNICEF, New Delhi, August 1990

10 Most of the information in this panel is taken from Cornia G.A. and Sipos, S., *Children and the Transition to the Market Economy: Safety Nets and Social Policies in Central and Eastern Europe*, UNICEF, International Child Development Centre, Florence, 1991

11 Private memorandum in connection with the UNICEF mission to Albania, July 1991

12 Because of the recession, the figure for 1990 (released after this report goes to press) may reach 23% or 24%

13 Johnson, C.M., Miranda, L., Sherman, A. and Weill, J.D., *Child Poverty in America,* Children's Defense Fund, 122 C Street, N.W., Washington, D.C. 20001

14 Much of the factual information in this panel is taken from *Effects of Armed Conflict on Women and Children: Relief and Rehabilitation in War Situations,* Vol. 10, Issue 2-3, 1991, Rehabilitation International and UNICEF, Technical Support Programme for the United Nations Decade of Disabled Persons (1983-1992)

15 UNICEF, Nairobi

16 The information in this panel is taken from *Ceara, North-East Brazil: Giving priority to the child at state level,* UNICEF, Brazil, May 1991

17 Wade, Robert, *Governing the Market: Economic Theory and Role of Governments in East Asian Industrialisation,* Princeton University Press, 1991

18 Berstecher D. and Carr-Hill, R., 'Primary education and economic recession in the developing world since 1980', a special study prepared for the World Conference on Education for All, Thailand, 5-9 March 1990, UNESCO, New York, 1990

19 Fredriksen, Birger, 'Increasing Foreign Aid for Primary Education: The Challenge to Donors', PHREE/90/30, World Bank, Education and Employment Division, Population and Human Resources Department, Washington, D.C., 1990

20 Oxenham, J. and de Jong, J., 'Improving the quality of education in developing countries', *Human Development in the 1990s and Beyond,* p. 121, United Nations, Department of International Economic and Social Affairs, New York, 1989

21 Colclough, C. and Lewin K., 'Educating all the children: the economic challenge for the 1990s', a summary paper for the World Conference on Education for All, Thailand, 5-9 March 1990, UNESCO, New York, 1990

22 Fredriksen, op. cit.

23 'Education: breakthrough in Bangladesh', *The State of the World's Children 1990,* P. 60, UNICEF, New York, 1989

24 Oxenham and de Jong, op. cit.

25 *Basic education and literacy: World statistical indicators,* UNESCO, Paris, 1990

26 ibid.

27 Berstecher and Carr-Hill, op. cit.

28 Most of the information in this panel is taken from McGinn, N.F., Snodgrass, R., Kim, Y.B. and Kim, S-B., *Education and Development in Korea,* chapter 5, p. 185, Harvard University Press, 1980

29 *Innocenti Declaration,* produced by participants at the WHO/UNICEF policy makers' meeting on Breastfeeding in the 1990s: A Global Initiative, Spedale degli Innocenti, Florence, 30 July-1 August 1990

30 Victora, C.G., Smith, P.G., Vaughan, J.P. et al. 'Evidence for protection by breastfeeding against deaths from infectious diseases in Brazil', *The Lancet,* 8 August 1987, No. 8554 319-22

31 From: 'Protecting, Promoting, and Supporting Breastfeeding: The Special Role of Maternity Services'. A joint WHO/UNICEF statement, WHO, Geneva

32 The worldwide campaign was launched at the International Conference on Breastfeeding hosted by UNICEF, WHO and the International Pediatric Association, 28 June 1991

33 'China: Putting Prevention First', *World Immunization News,* Vol. 5, No. 4, July-August 1989

34 'Financing Child Immunization in China', *World Immunization News,* Vol. 4, No. 3, May-June, 1988

35 Declaration of New York: the Children's Vaccine Initiative, WHO, Geneva, September 1990

36 ibid.

37 EPI Update, WHO, Geneva, March 1991

38 Expanded Programme on Immunization, Global Advisory Group report, WHO/EPI/Gen/91.3, WHO, Geneva, 1991

39 Participation in the Children's Vacine Initiative, recommendation to the UNICEF Executive Board, E/ICEF/1991/P/L.31, UNICEF, New York, 15 February 1991

40 Programme of action for achieving the goals for children and development in the 1990s, E/ICEF/1991/12, UNICEF, New York, 22 March 1991

41 *Glimpse,* newsletter of the International Centre for Diarrhoeal Disease Research, Bangladesh, Vol. 11, No. 3, May-June 1989

42 Kane, Dr. M.A., Clements Dr C.J. and Hu, Dr. D.J., 'Integration of Hepatitis B Vaccine into the EPI', meeting of the WHO Global Advisory Group on EPI, Cairo, Egypt, 14-18 October 1990

43 *World Immunization News,* Vol. 6, No. 5, September-October 1990

44 'Hepatitis B Vaccine: Attacking an Epidemic',. EPI, WHO Update, WHO, Geneva, November 1989

45 Sample copies of *Facts for Life* and its companion booklet *All for Health* can be obtained by writing to UNICEF House, H-11F, *Facts for Life Unit,* 3 UN Plaza, New York, NY 10017, USA

II

STATISTICS

Economic and social statistics on the nations of the world, with particular reference to children's well-being.

General note on data   Signs and explanations

INDEX TO COUNTRIES

TABLES

1: Basic indicators

U5MR ☐ IMR ☐ population ☐ births and under five deaths ☐ GNP per capita ☐ life expectancy ☐ adult literacy ☐ school enrolment ☐ income distribution

2: Nutrition

Low birth weight ☐ breastfeeding ☐ malnutrition ☐ food production ☐ calorie intake ☐ food spending

3: Health

Access to water ☐ access to health services ☐ immunization of children and pregnant women ☐ ORT use

4: Education

Male and female literacy ☐ radio and television sets ☐ primary school enrolment and completion ☐ secondary school enrolment

5: Demographic indicators

Child population ☐ population growth rate ☐ crude death rate ☐ crude birth rate ☐ life expectancy ☐ fertility rate ☐ urbanization

6: Economic indicators

GNP per capita and annual growth rates ☐ inflation ☐ poverty ☐ government expenditure ☐ aid ☐ debt service

7: Women

Life expectancy ☐ literacy ☐ enrolment in school ☐ contraceptive use ☐ tetanus immunization ☐ trained attendance at births ☐ maternal mortality

8: Basic indicators on less populous countries

9: The rate of progress

U5MR reduction rates ☐ GNP per capita growth rates ☐ fertility reduction rates

Footnotes to tables 1-9   Definitions   Main sources

General note on the data

The data provided in these tables are accompanied by definitions, sources, explanations of signs and individual footnotes where the definition of the datum is different from the general definition being used. Tables derived from so many sources - eleven major sources are listed in the explanatory material - will inevitably cover a wide range of data reliability. Official government data received by the responsible United Nations agency have been used whenever possible. In the many cases where there are no reliable official figures, estimates made by the responsible United Nations agency have been used. Where such internationally standardized estimates do not exist, the tables draw on other sources, particularly data received from the appropriate UNICEF field office. Except for the indicators of under five mortality rate (U5MR), access to safe water, access to health services and the indicators of immunization coverage, where UNICEF is identified as a main source, all UNICEF estimates are marked with an * or a y.

Where possible only comprehensive or representative national data have been used. Where the data refer to only a part of the country this is indicated in a footnote.

The data for infant mortality rates, life expectancy, crude birth and death rates, etc. are part of the regular work on estimates and projections undertaken by the United Nations Population Division. These and other internationally produced estimates are revised periodically, which explains why some of the data will differ from those found in earlier UNICEF publications. In the case of GNP per capita and ODA, the data are the result of a continuous process of revising and updating by the World Bank and OECD respectively. The tables this year include extensive revisions to the data on literacy, underweight, wasting, stunting, access to water and maternal mortality.

The value of 70 under five deaths per 1000 live births used to delineate the two higher U5MR groups of countries from the two lower groups reflects the World Summit for Children mortality goal target. The U5MR goal aims at a reduction of the under five mortality rate in all countries during the 1990s by one-third or to 70 per 1000 live births, whichever is less. Hence, if all countries achieve the under five mortality goal, by the end of the 1990s all countries should belong to the two lowest U5MR groups.

Signs and explanations

Unless otherwise stated, the summary measures for the four U5MR (under five mortality rate) groups of countries are the median values for each group. The median is the middle value of a data set arranged in order of magnitude. It is the measure commonly used

where there are a large number of items of data with a great range, as is the case in these tables, and it has the advantage of not being distorted by the very small or the very large countries.

. .   Data not available

*   UNICEF estimate

T   Total (as opposed to a median).

x   See footnote at the end of the tables

y   UNICEF estimate; see footnote at the end of the tables.

U5MR estimates for individual countries are derived from data produced by the UN Population Division on an internationally comparable basis using various sources. In some cases, these estimates may differ from the latest national figures. In general, data released during approximately the last two years are not incorporated in these estimates.

More information on the derivation of the U5MR figures can be obtained by writing to G.Jones, Senior Adviser, Statistics and Monitoring, UNICEF, 3 U.N. Plaza, New York, NY 10017, U.S.A.

Index to countries

In the following tables, countries are ranked in descending order of their estimated 1990 under five mortality rate. The reference numbers indicating that rank are given in the alphabetical list of countries below.

TABLE 1: BASIC INDICATORS

		Under 5 mortality rate		Infant mortality rate (under 1)		Total population (millions) 1990	Annual no. of births (thousands) 1990	Annual no. of under 5 deaths (thousands) 1990	GNP per capita (US $) 1989	Life expectancy at birth (years) 1990	Total adult literacy rate 1990	% of age group enrolled in primary school Total 1986-1989	% share of household income 1980-1988	
		1960	1990	1960	1990								lowest 40%	highest 20%
	Very high U5MR countries (over 140) Median	**302**	**189**	**184**	**116**	**1536T**	**58458T**	**9774T**	**290**	**50**	**35**	**63**	**. .**	**. .**
1	Mozambique	331	**297**	190	173	15.7	699	208	80	48	33	68	. .	. .
2	Afghanistan	381	**292**	215	167	16.6	888	260	280ˣ	43	29	25	. .	. .
3	Angola	344	**292**	208	173	10.0	472	138	610	46	42	93	. .	. .
4	Mali	369	**284**	210	164	9.2	472	134	270	45	32	23	. .	. .
5	Sierra Leone	385	**257**	219	149	4.2	201	52	220	42	21	53	. .	. .
6	Malawi	366	**253**	207	144	8.8	494	125	180	48	. .	72	. .	. .
7	Guinea-Bissau	336	**246**	200	146	1.0	41	10	180	43	. .	53	. .	. .
8	Guinea	336	**237**	203	140	5.8	294	70	430	44	24	30	. .	. .
9	Burkina Faso	363	**228**	205	133	9.0	426	97	320	48	18	32	. .	. .
10	Niger	321	**221**	191	130	7.7	401	89	290	46	28	30	. .	. .
11	Ethiopia	294	**220**	175	130	49.2	2424	534	120	46	. .	36	. .	. .
12	Chad	325	**216**	195	127	5.7	249	54	190	47	30	51	. .	. .
13	Somalia	294	**215**	175	127	7.5	360	77	170	46	17ˣ	15	. .	. .
14	Mauritania	321	**214**	191	122	2.0	94	20	500	47	34	52	. .	. .
15	Liberia	310	**205**	184	134	2.6	122	25	450ˣ	54	40	34	. .	. .
16	Rwanda	248	**198**	146	117	7.2	368	73	320	50	50	67	. .	. .
17	Cambodia	218	**193**	146	123	8.2	322	62	. .	50	35	. .	. .	. .
18	Burundi	260	**192**	153	115	5.5	261	50	220	49	50	59	. .	. .
19	Bhutan	298	**189**	187	123	1.5	58	11	190ˣ	49	38	26	. .	. .
20	Nepal	298	**189**	187	123	19.1	725	137	180	52	26	86	13ˣ	59ˣ
21	Yemen	378	**187**	214	114	11.7	602	113	650	51	32ʸ	87	. .	. .
22	Senegal	299	**185**	172	84	7.3	328	61	650	48	38	59	. .	. .
23	Bangladesh	262	**180**	156	114	115.6	4796	866	180	52	35	70	24	37
24	Madagascar	364	**176**	220	115	12.0	547	96	230	55	80	97	. .	. .
25	Sudan	292	**172**	170	104	25.2	1111	191	420ˣ	51	27	49	. .	. .
26	Tanzania	249	**170**	147	102	27.3	1387	235	130	54	91ʸ	66	. .	. .
27	Central African Rep.	08	**169**	183	100	3.0	138	23	390	50	38	67	. .	. .
28	Namibia	263	**167**	155	102	1.8	76	13	1030	58	. .	. .	. .	. .
29	Nigeria	316	**167**	190	101	108.5	5183	865	250	52	51	66	. .	. .
30	Gabon	287	**164**	171	99	1.2	49	8	2960	53	61	. .	. .	. .
31	Uganda	223	**164**	133	99	18.8	985	161	250	52	48	77	. .	. .
32	Bolivia	282	**160**	167	102	7.3	309	50	620	55	78	91	12*	58*
33	Pakistan	276	**158**	163	104	122.6	5451	863	370	58	35	40	19	46
34	Laos	233	**152**	155	104	4.1	187	28	180	50	. .	110	. .	. .
35	Cameroon	275	**148**	163	90	11.8	566	83	1000	54	54	111	. .	. .
36	Benin	310	**147**	185	88	4.6	229	34	380	47	23	63	. .	. .
37	Togo	305	**147**	182	90	3.5	158	23	390	54	43	101	. .	. .
38	India	282	**142**	165	94	853.1	26985	3835	340	59	48	99	20	41
	High U5MR countries (71-140) Median	**229**	**90**	**143**	**66**	**793T**	**25837T**	**2510T**	**885**	**62**	**68**	**97**	**12**	**55**
39	Ghana	224	**140**	132	86	15.0	665	93	390	55	60	73	17	45
40	Côte d'Ivoire	264	**136**	165	92	12.0	603	82	790	53	54	70	13	53
41	Haiti	270	**130**	182	92	6.5	233	30	360	56	53	83	6*	48*
42	Zaire	269	**130**	158	79	35.6	1626	211	260	53	72	76	. .	. .
43	Lesotho	208	**129**	149	95	1.8	72	9	470	57	. .	112	. .	. .
44	Zambia	228	**122**	135	76	8.5	433	53	390	54	73	97	11ˣ	61ˣ
45	Peru	233	**116**	142	82	21.6	647	75	1010	63	85	122	13	52
46	Libyan Arab Jamahiriya	269	**112**	160	75	4.5	199	22	5310	62	64	. .	. .	. .
47	Morocco	265	**112**	163	75	25.1	858	96	880	62	50	67	23	39
48	Congo	241	**110**	143	69	2.3	105	12	940	54	57	. .	. .	. .
49	Kenya	208	**108**	124	68	24.0	1132	122	360	60	69	93	9ˣ	60ˣ
50	Algeria	270	**98**	168	68	25.0	877	86	2230	65	57	96	. .	. .
51	Indonesia	225	**97**	139	71	184.3	5091	494	500	61	77	119	21	41
52	Guatemala	230	**94**	125	54	9.2	367	34	910	63	55	77	14	55
53	Saudi Arabia	292	**91**	170	65	14.1	594	54	6020	65	62	71	. .	. .
54	South Africa	192	**88**	135	67	35.3	1108	98	2470	62	. .	. .	. .	. .
55	Myanmar	230	**88**	153	65	41.7	1252	111	220ˣ	61	81	103	. .	. .
56	El Salvador	207	**87**	143	59	5.3	191	17	1070	64	73	80	8*	66*
57	Zimbabwe	181	**87**	110	61	9.7	399	35	650	60	67	128	. .	. .
58	Iraq	222	**86**	139	63	18.9	789	68	2340ˣ	65	60	96	. .	. .
59	Egypt	301	**85**	179	61	52.4	1727	148	640	60	48	90	21*	41*
60	Botswana	173	**85**	119	63	1.3	61	5	1600	60	74	117	9	59
61	Turkey	258	**80**	190	69	55.9	1579	134	1370	65	81	117	11*	55*
62	Mongolia	185	**84**	128	64	2.2	77	7	780ˣ	63	. .	102	. .	. .
63	Honduras	232	**84**	144	63	5.1	198	17	900	65	73	106	12*	59*

Note: nations are listed in descending order of their 1990 under five mortality rates (shown in bold type).

		Under 5 mortality rate		Infant mortality rate (under 1)		Total population (millions) 1990	Annual no. of births (thousands) 1990	Annual no. of under 5 deaths (thousands) 1990	GNP per capita (US $) 1989	Life expectancy at birth (years) 1990	Total adult literacy rate 1990	% of age group enrolled in primary school Total 1986-1989	% share of household income 1980-1988	
		1960	1990	1960	1990								lowest 40%	highest 20%
64	Ecuador	184	**83**	124	60	10.6	338	28	1020	66	86	117	. .	. .
65	Brazil	159	**83**	116	60	150.4	4115	341	2540	66	81	104	8	63
66	Papua New Guinea	248	**80**	165	56	3.9	131	10	890	55	52	73	. .	. .
67	Nicaragua	209	**78**	140	56	3.9	156	1	830ˣ	65	. .	99	12*	58*
68	Dominican Rep.	199	**78**	125	61	7.2	214	17	790	67	83	101	. .	. .
	Middle U5MR countries (21-70) Median	**134**	**35**	**86**	**30**	**2048T**	**45680T**	**1909T**	**1775**	**70**	**88**	**105**	**14**	**51**
69	Philippines	134	**69**	80	43	62.4	1988	138	710	64	90	110	14*	52*
70	Viet Nam	232	**65**	156	49	66.7	2076	134	240ˣ	63	88	101	. .	. .
71	Tunisia	254	**62**	159	48	8.2	239	15	1260	67	65	113	. .	. .
72	Paraguay	134	**60**	86	41	4.3	146	9	1030	67	90	104	. .	. .
73	Syria	217	**59**	135	44	12.5	550	33	980	66	65	110	. .	. .
74	Iran, Islamic Rep. of	254	**59**	169	46	54.6	1830	36	3200	66	54	116	. .	. .
75	Lebanon	91	**56**	68	44	2.7	85	5	2150ˣ	66	80	125	. .	. .
76	Jordan	217	**52**	135	40	4.0	157	8	1640	67	80	99	. .	. .
77	Colombia	157	**50**	99	39	33.0	878	44	1200	69	87	114	13	53
78	Mexico	140	**49**	92	40	88.6	2466	122	2010	70	87	117	13*	. .
79	Oman	378	**49**	214	37	1.5	67	3	5220	66	. .	100	. .	. .
80	Venezuela	114	**43**	81	35	19.7	582	25	2450	70	88	106	14	51
81	China	203	**42**	150	30	1139.1	24288	1010	350	70	73	134	22*	38*
82	Albania	151	**37**	112	31	3.2	74	3	. .	72	. .	100	. .	. .
83	Argentina	75	**35**	61	31	32.3	670	24	2160	71	95	111	. .	. .
84	Korea, Dem.	120	**35**	85	26	21.8	530	18	970ˣ	70	. .	100	. .	. .
85	Sri Lanka	114	**35**	71	26	17.2	369	13	430	71	88	107	13	56
86	Thailand	149	**34**	103	26	55.7	1158	39	1220	66	93	96	15ˣ	50ˣ
87	Romania	82	**34**	69	27	23.3	358	12	1620ˣ	71	. .	97	. .	. .
88	USSR	53	**31**	38	23	288.6	5065	159	4550ˣ	71	. .	105	. .	. .
89	Panama	105	**31**	69	22	2.4	63	2	1760	72	88	106	. .	. .
90	United Arab Emirates	239	**30**	145	24	1.6	34	1	18430	70	48*	104	. .	. .
91	Korea, Rep.	120	**30**	85	23	42.8	670	20	4400	70	96	108	20*	42*
92	Malaysia	105	**29**	73	22	17.9	538	16	2160	70	78	102	14	51
93	Mauritius	104	**28**	70	22	1.1	19	1	1990	70	. .	105	12*	46*
94	Chile	143	**27**	114	20	13.2	306	8	1770	72	93	100	13*	54*
95	Uruguay	57	**25**	51	22	3.1	54	1	2620	72	96	100	18*	44*
96	Yugoslavia	113	**23**	82	20	23.8	339	8	2920	73	93	95	17	43
97	Costa Rica	121	**22**	84	18	3.0	81	2	1780	75	93	100	12	55
	Low U5MR countries (20 and under) Median	**39**	**10**	**32**	**8**	**896T**	**11829T**	**126T**	**14485**	**76**	**. .**	**102**	**18**	**40**
98	Jamaica	89	**20**	63	16	2.5	56	1	1260	73	98	103	15	49
99	Kuwait	128	**19**	89	17	2.0	55	1	16150	73	73	93	. .	. .
100	Poland	70	**18**	62	16	38.4	588	11	1790	72	. .	101	24	35
101	Bulgaria	69	**18**	49	14	9.0	112	2	2320	73	. .	104	. .	. .
102	Trinidad and Tobago	67	**17**	54	15	1.3	32	1	3230	72	. .	100	13ˣ	50ˣ
103	Hungary	57	**16**	51	15	10.6	123	2	2590	71	. .	97	26	32
104	Portugal	112	**16**	81	13	10.3	137	2	4250	74	85	127	. .	. .
105	Cuba	87	**14**	62	11	10.6	188	3	1170ˣ	75	94	104	. .	. .
106	Czechoslovakia	33	**13**	27	11	15.7	217	3	3450	72	. .	96	. .	. .
107	New Zealand	26	**12**	23	10	3.4	55	1	12070	75	. .	107	16	45
108	Israel	39	**11**	33	10	4.6	99	1	9790	76	. .	95	18ˣ	40ˣ
109	Greece	64	**11**	53	10	10.0	117	1	5350	76	93	106	. .	. .
110	USA	29	**11**	26	9	249.2	3634	40	20910	76	. .	100	16	42
111	Italy	50	**10**	44	9	57.1	587	6	15120	76	97	95	19	41
112	Norway	22	**10**	19	8	4.2	53	1	22290	77	. .	95	19	38
113	Australia	24	**10**	21	8	16.9	246	2	14360	77	. .	106	16	42
114	Spain	57	**10**	47	8	39.2	486	5	9330	77	95	113	19	40
115	Belgium	35	**9**	31	8	9.8	118	1	16220	75	. .	100	22ˣ	36ˣ
116	Austria	43	**9**	37	8	7.6	88	1	17300	75	. .	101	. .	. .
117	United Kingdom	27	**9**	23	8	57.2	786	7	14610	76	. .	106	17ˣ	40ˣ
118	Singapore	49	**9**	36	8	2.7	47	0	10450	74	. .	109	15	49
119	France	34	**9**	29	8	56.1	761	7	17820	76	. .	113	18ˣ	41ˣ
120	Switzerland	26	**9**	22	7	6.6	78	1	29880	77	. .	. .	17	45
121	Denmark	25	**9**	22	8	5.1	57	1	20450	76	. .	99	17	39
122	Ireland	36	**9**	31	8	3.7	67	1	8710	75	. .	100	. .	. .
123	Germany	40	**9**	34	7	77.6	863	8	20440ˣ	75	. .	105	20ˣ	39ˣ
124	Canada	33	**9**	28	7	26.5	356	3	19030	77	. .	105	18	40
125	Netherlands	21	**9**	18	7	15.0	192	2	15920	77	. .	115	20	38
126	Hong Kong	64	**7**	44	7	5.9	72	1	10350	77	. .	106	16	47
127	Finland	28	**7**	22	6	5.0	60	0	22120	75	. .	101	18	38
128	Sweden	20	**7**	16	6	8.4	109	1	21570	77	. .	100	21	37
129	Japan	39	**6**	31	5	123.5	1390	9	23810	79	. .	102	22ˣ	38ˣ

TABLE 2: NUTRITION

		% of infants with low birth-weight 1980-88	% of mothers breast-feeding 1980-91			% of children (1980-91) suffering from:				Average index of food production per capita (1979-81=100) 1990	Daily per capita calorie supply as % of requirements 1988	% of household income (1980-85) spent on:	
			3 months	6 months	12 months	underweight (0-4 years) moderate & severe	severe	wasting (12-23 months) moderate & severe	stunting (24-59 months) moderate & severe			all food	cereals
	Very high U5MR countries (over 140) Median	**17**	**93**	**90**	**82**	**33**	**6**	**14**	**43**	**90**	**92**	**54**	**22**
1	Mozambique	20*	99*	96*	. .	. .	. .	. .	. .	85	70	. .	. .
2	Afghanistan	20	. .	74x	61x	. .	. .	. .	. .	. .	94x	. .	. .
3	Angola	17	. .	. .	. .	31x	. .	16	. .	77	73	. .	. .
4	Mali	17*	91	95	82	31x	9x	16	34x	96	93	57	22
5	Sierra Leone	17*	99*	98*	92*	23x	2x	14x	. .	88	79	56	22
6	Malawi	20*	. .	. .	96*	24x	. .	8	61	80	87	55	28
7	Guinea-Bissau	13	100	100	98	23x	. .	. .	. .	101	92	. .	. .
8	Guinea	25*	100*	90*	85*	. .	. .	. .	. .	87	88	. .	. .
9	Burkina Faso	21x	98*	98*	97*	. .	. .	. .	. .	108	87	. .	. .
10	Niger	15	65	30	15	49	. .	23x	38x	73	100	. .	. .
11	Ethiopia	8	. .	97*	95*	38x	. .	19x	43x	85	71	50	24
12	Chad	. .	. .	. .	. .	. .	. .	. .	. .	94	78	. .	. .
13	Somalia	. .	92*	78*	54*	. .	. .	. .	. .	96	75	. .	. .
14	Mauritania	11	91	86	67	31	. .	24x	37x	85	109	. .	. .
15	Liberia	. .	87	75	61	. .	. .	. .	. .	72	98	. .	. .
16	Rwanda	. .	97*	97*	74*	33x	4x	1x	34x	73	77	30	11
17	Cambodia	. .	100*	93*	72*	. .	. .	. .	. .	160	98x	. .	. .
18	Burundi	9x	. .	95*	90*	38x	10x	10	60x	89	97	. .	. .
19	Bhutan	. .	. .	. .	. .	38x	. .	4x	56x	86	. .	. .	. .
20	Nepal	. .	92x	92x	82x	. .	. .	. .	. .	109	94	57	38
21	Yemen	. .	74x	66x	34x	53x	. .	15x	61x	79	92	. .	. .
22	Senegal	11	95	91	86	22x	6x	8	28x	100	84	50	15
23	Bangladesh	47	91x	86x	82x	66x	27x	28	66	99	83	59	36
24	Madagascar	10*	95	95	85	33x	8x	17	56x	90	93	59	26
25	Sudan	15*	93	90	79	. .	. .	13x	32x	67	85	60	. .
26	Tanzania	14	100*	90*	70*	48*	6*	. .	. .	85	93	64	32
27	Central African Rep.	15*	. .	. .	. .	. .	. .	. .	. .	95	88	. .	. .
28	Namibia	. .	98x	88x	73x	29x	6x	9x	30x	95	83	. .	. .
29	Nigeria	20*	98	97	92	36	12	16	60	113	86	52	18
30	Gabon	. .	. .	. .	. .	. .	. .	. .	. .	80	102	. .	. .
31	Uganda	. .	92	88	85	23	5	4	25x	90	86	. .	. .
32	Bolivia	12*	92	84	67	13x	3x	2	51x	105	87	33	. .
33	Pakistan	25*	87*	74*	70*	52x	10x	17x	42x	105	95	54	17
34	Laos	39	. .	99y	93y	37	. .	20	44	130	119	. .	. .
35	Cameroon	13x	92x	90x	77x	17x	. .	2x	43x	88	93	24	8
36	Benin	8*	90	90	76	. .	. .	. .	. .	115	93	37	12
37	Togo	20*	95	87	84	24	6	10	37x	96	93	. .	. .
38	India	30	. .	. .	. .	61x	9x	. .	. .	118	95	52	18
	High U5MR countries (71-140) Median	**14**	**90**	**82**	**76**	**16**	**2**	**4**	**34**	**94**	**105**	**40**	**12**
39	Ghana	17*	90	92	87	27	6	15	39	102	96	66	. .
40	Côte d'Ivoire	14x	87	84	78	12	2	17	20	92	102	40	14
41	Haiti	17x	92x	80*	. .	37x	3x	17x	51x	89	85	. .	. .
42	Zaire	13	100*	100*	86*	. .	. .	. .	. .	95	92	55	15
43	Lesotho	11	93x	89x	76x	16	2	7	23	76	101	. .	. .
44	Zambia	. .	. .	. .	93*	25x	5x	10x	59x	86	88	37	8
45	Peru	9*	85	76	58	13x	2x	3	43	90	97	35	8
46	Libyan Arab Jamahiriya	. .	. .	. .	. .	. .	. .	. .	. .	102	143	. .	. .
47	Morocco	. .	87	77	59	16x	4x	6	34x	124	117	40	12
48	Congo	16*	100*	98*	90*	24	. .	13	33	92	113	42	19
49	Kenya	15	94	92	82	. .	. .	10x	41x	108	85	39	16
50	Algeria	9*	. .	. .	. .	10x	. .	4x	13x	94	114	. .	. .
51	Indonesia	14	95	87	79	51x	1x	. .	. .	132	124	61	18
52	Guatemala	14*	95	79	80	34x	8x	3	68x	95	107	36	10
53	Saudi Arabia	6	91*	52*	. .	. .	. .	. .	. .	252	117	. .	. .
54	South Africa	12	. .	. .	. .	. .	. .	. .	. .	85	124	26	. .
55	Myanmar	16*	90	90	90	38x	. .	17	75x	96	119	. .	. .
56	El Salvador	15*	85	77	55	15	. .	3	36	94	105	33	12
57	Zimbabwe	. .	95	92	88	12x	2x	2	31x	92	93	40	9
58	Iraq	9*	76	45	19	. .	. .	. .	. .	92	123	. .	. .
59	Egypt	5	90	83	68	13x	3x	2	32x	123	128	50	10
60	Botswana	8*	97	90	73	15	. .	. .	51x	75	98	35	13
61	Turkey	7*	98*	72*	63*	. .	. .	. .	. .	98	122	40	8
62	Mongolia	10	70*	. .	. .	. .	. .	. .	. .	88	101	. .	. .
63	Honduras	20*	73*	55*	. .	21	4	2x	34x	89	96	39	. .

Note: nations are listed in descending order of their 1990 under five mortality rates (see table 1).

| | | % of infants with low birth-weight 1980-88 | % of mothers breast-feeding 1980-91 | | | % of children (1980-91) suffering from: | | | | Average index of food production per capita (1979-81=100) 1990 | Daily per capita calorie supply as % of requirements 1988 | % of household income (1980-85) spent on: | |
			3 months	6 months	12 months	underweight (0-4 years) moderate & severe	severe	wasting (12-23 months) moderate & severe	stunting (24-59 months) moderate & severe			all food	cereals
64	Ecuador	11*	84	73	57	17	0	4	39	107	102	30	..
65	Brazil	8*	66x	37x	34x	7	1	3	16	105	113	35	9
66	Papua New Guinea	25x	..	..	..	35	..	..	..	105	98	..	..
67	Nicaragua	15	..	..	..	11	1	0	22	62	105	..	..
68	Dominican Rep.	16*	70	47	25	13x	2x	3	26x	91	104	46	13
	Middle U5MR countries (21-70) Median	**8**	**81**	**57**	**38**	**19**	**3**	**7**	**23**	**99**	**120**	**35**	**7**
69	Philippines	18*	..	74*	..	34	5	14	45	88	100	51	20
70	Viet Nam	17*	96*	93*	49*	42	14	12x	49x	123	103	..	..
71	Tunisia	8*	92	76	58	10x	2x	4	23x	102	124	37	7
72	Paraguay	7	85	69	45	4	1	0	17	120	122	30	6
73	Syria	11*	81*	72*	..	..	..	..	..	82	128	..	..
74	Iran, Islamic Rep. of	5	91*	73*	51*	43x	..	23x	55x	97	129	37	10
75	Lebanon	10	50*	40*	15*	..	..	..	..	..	125	..	..
76	Jordan	5x	93	80	61	..	..	..	..	108	118	35	..
77	Colombia	8*	80	56	36	10	2	5	18	111	110	29	..
78	Mexico	12*	71	50	33	14	..	6x	22x	97	135	35	..
79	Oman	7*	75*	55*	20*	..	..	..	..	..	..	..	..
80	Venezuela	9	50x	40x	30x	6x	..	4x	7x	92	103	38	..
81	China	9*	65*	55*	..	21x	3x	8x	41x	138	112	61	..
82	Albania	7	..	..	..	..	..	..	..	93	114x	..	..
83	Argentina	..	66	36	14	..	..	..	..	92	133	35	4
84	Korea, Dem.	..	..	..	..	..	..	..	..	107	135	..	..
85	Sri Lanka	25*	94	80	72	38x	9x	19	34x	89	104	43	18
86	Thailand	12	89	69	67	26x	4x	10	28x	101	103	30	7
87	Romania	6	..	..	..	..	..	..	..	91	127	..	..
88	USSR	6	..	..	..	..	..	..	..	112	133x	..	..
89	Panama	8	62	53	55	16	..	7	24	90	107	38	7
90	United Arab Emirates	6*	..	..	..	..	..	..	..	..	..	..	..
91	Korea, Rep.	9	58x	40x	27x	..	..	..	..	89	122	35	14
92	Malaysia	10	88	..	..	..	..	..	..	159	120	30	..
93	Mauritius	9*	79	55	40	24	..	16x	22x	105	118	24	7
94	Chile	7	81*	57*	20*	3x	..	1	10x	118	106	29	7
95	Uruguay	8*	50*	40*	..	7x	2x	..	16x	110	104	31	7
96	Yugoslavia	7	..	..	..	..	..	..	..	88	138	27	..
97	Costa Rica	6*	85*	60*	24*	6	..	3	8	92	124	33	8
	Low U5MR countries (20 and under) Median	**6**	**47**	**25**	**..**	**..**	**..**	**..**	**..**	**103**	**132**	**16**	**2**
98	Jamaica	8*	95	82	43	7	1	6	7	89	115	39	..
99	Kuwait	5*	47x	32x	12y	0	..	2	14	..	..	..	..
100	Poland	8	32x	25x	..	..	..	..	..	108	132	29	..
101	Bulgaria	6	..	..	..	..	..	..	..	95	145	..	..
102	Trinidad and Tobago	..	84	49	27	7x	0x	5	4x	69	122	..	..
103	Hungary	10	86	..	..	..	..	..	..	107	137	25	..
104	Portugal	5	29	12	7	..	..	..	..	121	138	34	..
105	Cuba	8	..	..	..	..	..	1x	..	98	135	..	..
106	Czechoslovakia	6	..	..	..	..	..	..	..	122	144	..	..
107	New Zealand	5	..	..	..	..	..	..	..	99	131	12	2
108	Israel	7	..	..	..	..	..	..	..	99	122	22	..
109	Greece	6	..	..	..	..	..	..	..	95	148	30	..
110	USA	7	33	24	..	..	..	..	..	96	139	13	2
111	Italy	..	..	..	..	..	..	..	..	94	142	19	2
112	Norway	4	..	..	..	..	..	..	..	100	121	15	2
113	Australia	6x	56	40	10	..	..	..	..	95	125	13	2
114	Spain	1	..	..	..	..	..	..	..	114	144	24	3
115	Belgium	5	..	..	..	..	..	..	..	119	146x	15	2
116	Austria	6	41	..	..	..	..	..	..	105	132	16	2
117	United Kingdom	7	26	22	..	..	..	..	..	109	129	12	2
118	Singapore	6	..	..	..	14x	..	..	..	94	126	19	..
119	France	5	..	..	..	..	..	..	..	99	131	16	2
120	Switzerland	5x	..	..	..	..	..	..	..	103	132	17	..
121	Denmark	6	..	..	..	..	..	..	..	138	133	13	2
122	Ireland	4	..	..	..	..	..	..	..	114	147	22	4
123	Germany	6	..	..	..	..	..	..	..	114	..	..	..
124	Canada	6	53	30	..	..	..	..	..	115	130	11	2
125	Netherlands	..	33x	..	..	..	..	..	..	119	125	13	2
126	Hong Kong	5	..	..	..	..	..	..	..	67	127	12	1
127	Finland	4	..	7x	..	..	..	..	..	115	117	16	3
128	Sweden	4	47	23	..	..	..	..	..	104	112	13	2
129	Japan	5	..	..	..	..	..	..	..	95	122	16	4

TABLE 3: HEALTH

| | | % of population with access to safe water 1988-90 | | | % of population with access to health service 1985-90 | | | Percentage fully immunized 1981/1989-90 | | | | | |
| | | | | | | | | one-year-old children | | | | pregnant women Tetanus | ORT use rate 1987-89 |
		total	urban	rural	total	urban	rural	TB	DPT	Polio	Measles		
	Very high U5MR countries (over 140) **Median**	**42**	**66**	**34**	**46**	**88**	**38**	**24/85**	**14/55**	**8/54**	**23/55**	**5/44**	**27**
1	Mozambique	24	44	17	39	100	30	46/59	56/46	32/46	32/58	../25	30
2	Afghanistan	21	39	17	29	80	17	8/30	3/25	3/25	6/20	3/ 3	11
3	Angola	35	75	19	30ˣ	..	..	../47	../23	../23	../38	../26	12
4	Mali	41	53	38	15	..	..	19/82	../42	../42	../43	1/31	41
5	Sierra Leone	42	83	22	..	..	..	35/98	15/83	13/83	28/75	10/77	55
6	Malawi	56ˣ	97ˣ	50ˣ	80	..	..	86/97	66/81	68/79	65/80	../82	14
7	Guinea-Bissau	25	18	27	..	..	..	../90	../38	../38	../42	../44	5
8	Guinea	32	55	24	47	100	40	4/53	../17	../17	15/18	5/10	63
9	Burkina Faso	69	44	72	49ˣ	51ˣ	48ˣ	16/84	2/37	2/37	23/42	11/76	16
10	Niger	61	100	52	41	99	30	28/50	6/13	6/13	19/21	3/44	54
11	Ethiopia	19	70	11	46	..	..	10/57	6/44	7/44	7/37	../43	32
12	Chad	..	..	..	30	..	..	../59	../20	../20	../32	../42	10
13	Somalia	37	50	29	27ˣ	50ˣ	15ˣ	3/31	2/18	2/18	3/30	5/ 5	38
14	Mauritania	66	67	65	40	..	..	57/75	18/28	18/28	45/33	1/40	54
15	Liberia	55	93	22	39	50	30	87/62ˣ	39/28ˣ	26/28ˣ	99/55ˣ	60/20ˣ	9
16	Rwanda	50ˣ	79ˣ	48ˣ	27ˣ	40ˣ	25ˣ	51/92	17/84	15/83	42/83	5/87	24
17	Cambodia	3ˣ	10ˣ	2ˣ	53	80	50	../54	../40	../40	../34	./..	6
18	Burundi	38	100	34	61	..	..	65/97	38/86	6/86	30/75	25/56	30
19	Bhutan	32	60	30	65	..	..	36/99	13/95	11/95	21/89	../63	40
20	Nepal	37	66	34	..	..	..	32/97	16/79	1/78	2/67	4/28	14
21	Yemen	38ˣ	56ˣ	30ˣ	38	..	..	14/71	21/53	21/53	33/45	../ 8	7
22	Senegal	54ˣ	79ˣ	38ˣ	40	..	..	../92	../60	../66	../59	../45	27
23	Bangladesh	81	39	89	45	..	..	1/86	1/62	1/62	../54	1/74	26
24	Madagascar	22	62	10	56	..	..	25/67	40/46	../46	../33	../60	11
25	Sudan	46	56	43	51	90	40	3/73	1/62	1/62	1/57	1/14	36
26	Tanzania	56	75	46	76ˣ	99ˣ	72ˣ	78/93	58/85	49/82	76/83	36/42	37
27	Central African Rep.	12	13	11	45	..	..	../96	../82	../82	../82	../87	20
28	Namibia	..	..	..	..	..	..	../85	../53	../53	../41	../50	..
29	Nigeria	..	..	54	66	85	62	23/96	24/57	24/57	55/54	11/58	35
30	Gabon	68	90	50	90ˣ	..	..	../96	../78	../78	../76	../86	10
31	Uganda	21	43	18	61ˣ	90ˣ	57ˣ	18/99	9/77	8/77	22/74	20/31	15
32	Bolivia	53	77	27	63	90	36	30/48	13/41	15/50	17/53	../20	60
33	Pakistan	56	80	45	55	99	35	11/98	3/96	3/96	2/97	1/87	42
34	Laos	29	47	25	67	..	..	4/26	7/18	7/26	7/13	2/10	30
35	Cameroon	44	50	39	41	44	39	8/76	5/56	5/54	16/56	../63	22
36	Benin	54	66	46	18	..	..	../92	../67	../67	../70	../83	45
37	Togo	71	100	61	61	..	..	44/94	9/61	9/61	47/57	57/81	33
38	India	75	79	73	..	..	..	12/97	31/92	7/93	../87	24/77	13
	High U5MR countries (71-140) **Median**	**61**	**85**	**41**	**75**	**97**	**50**	**61/83**	**42/75**	**42/76**	**33/73**	**10/48**	**45**
39	Ghana	57	93	39	60	92	45	67/81	22/57	25/56	23/60	11/33	21
40	Côte d'Ivoire	..	..	..	30ˣ	61ˣ	11ˣ	70/63	42/48	34/48	28/42	25/63	16
41	Haiti	36	59	27	50	..	..	60/72	14/41	3/40	../31	../23	24
42	Zaire	33	59	17	26	40	17	34/65	18/32	18/31	23/31	../29	40
43	Lesotho	48	59	45	80	..	..	81/97	56/76	54/75	49/76	./..	68
44	Zambia	60	76	43	75ˣ	100ˣ	50ˣ	72/97	44/79	77/78	21/76	../68	87
45	Peru	61	78	22	75ˣ	..	..	63/83	18/72	18/73	24/64	4/ 9	25
46	Libyan Arab Jamahiriya	94	100	80	..	..	..	55/90	55/84	55/84	57/70	6/ 6	60
47	Morocco	61	100	25	70	100	50	../94	43/81	45/81	../79	../64	14
48	Congo	38	92	2	83	97	70	92/90	42/79	42/79	49/75	../60	13
49	Kenya	31ˣ	61ˣ	21ˣ	..	..	..	../80	../74	../71	../59	../37	80
50	Algeria	71ˣ	85ˣ	55ˣ	88	100	80	59/99	33/89	30/89	17/83	../27	26
51	Indonesia	46	60	40	80	..	..	55/93	../87	../91	../86	10/41	39
52	Guatemala	61	91	41	34	47	25	29/62	42/66	42/74	8/68	1/48	24
53	Saudi Arabia	94	100	74	97	100	88	49/99	53/94	52/94	12/90	../62	45
54	South Africa	..	..	..	..	..	..	../85	../67	../69	../63	./..	..
55	Myanmar	33	43	29	33	100	11	15/66	5/61	../61	../44	6/56	19
56	El Salvador	48	84	19	56	80	40	47/60	42/76	38/76	44/75	20/12	45
57	Zimbabwe	66	31	80	71	100	62	64/71	39/73	38/72	56/69	../60	77
58	Iraq	92	100	72	93	97	78	76/96	13/75	16/75	33/62	4/67	70
59	Egypt	73ˣ	92ˣ	56ˣ	..	..	..	71/88	82/87	84/87	65/86	10/63	83
60	Botswana	54ˣ	84ˣ	46ˣ	89ˣ	100ˣ	85ˣ	80/92	64/86	71/82	68/78	32/62	66
61	Turkey	78ˣ	95ˣ	63ˣ	..	..	..	42/..	64/74	69/74	52/67	../15	..
62	Mongolia	65	78	50	..	..	..	53/92	99/84	99/85	../86	./..	59
63	Honduras	73	89	60	66	80	56	46/71	38/84	37/87	38/90	11/51	66

Note: nations are listed in descending order of their 1990 under five mortality rates (see table 1).

		% of population with access to safe water 1988-90			% of population with access to health service 1985-90			Percentage fully immunized 1981/1989-90				pregnant women Tetanus	ORT use rate 1987-89
								one-year-old children					
		total	urban	rural	total	urban	rural	TB	DPT	Polio	Measles		
64	Ecuador	58	75	37	75	92	40	82/88	26/68	19/67	31/61	4/ 8	70
65	Brazil	97	100	86	..	..	..	62/78	47/81	99/93	73/78	../62	45
66	Papua New Guinea	34	93	23	96	..	..	64/89	50/69	32/69	../67	../70	46
67	Nicaragua	54	78	19	83	100	60	65/81	23/65	52/86	20/82	../25	38
68	Dominican Rep.	63	86	28	80	..	..	34/68	27/69	42/90	17/96	26/24	22
	Middle U5MR countries (21-70) Median	**77**	**91**	**60**	**81**	**98**	**78**	**65/95**	**52/90**	**51/90**	**46/87**	**6/53**	**51**
69	Philippines	81	93	72	..	..	..	61/97	51/89	44/88	../85	37/47	25
70	Viet Nam	42	50	40	80	100	75	../90	../87	../87	../87	../18	65
71	Tunisia	68	100	31	90x	100x	80x	65/99	36/90	37/90	65/87	2/40	63
72	Paraguay	34	65	7	61	..	..	42/90	28/78	26/76	16/69	6/58	52
73	Syria	70	90	50	75x	92x	60x	36/92	14/90	14/90	14/87	3/84	67
74	Iran, Islamic Rep. of	89	98	76	80	95	65	6/95	29/93	47/91	48/83	2/47	71
75	Lebanon	..	..	..	..	..	..	../.	../82	../82	../39	../.	10
76	Jordan	99	100	98	97	98	95	../.	81/92	87/92	40/87	2/23	68
77	Colombia	88	88	87	60	..	..	57/95	20/87	22/93	26/82	6/40	40
78	Mexico	71	79	49	78	80	60	41/70	41/66	85/96	33/78	../42	72
79	Oman	47	87	42	91	100	90	49/93	9/96	9/96	6/96	27/97	19
80	Venezuela	90x	93x	65x	..	..	..	77/63	54/63	75/72	43/62	../.	49
81	China	74	87	68	90	100	80	../99	../97	../98	../98	../.	40
82	Albania	..	..	..	..	..	..	93/94	94/94	92/96	90/96	../.	..
83	Argentina	65	73	17	71	80	21	63/99	46/85	38/89	73/95	../.	70
84	Korea, Dem.	..	..	..	..	..	..	52/99	52/98	51/99	31/99	../99	52
85	Sri Lanka	60	80	55	93x	..	..	58/88	45/90	49/90	../83	48/60	58
86	Thailand	74	67	76	70	85	80	71/99	52/92	22/92	../80	27/79	40
87	Romania	..	..	..	..	..	..	../.	../96	../95	../79	../.	..
88	USSR	..	..	..	..	..	..	../02	06/68	06/76	05/86	../.	..
89	Panama	84	100	66	80x	95x	64x	77/97	49/86	50/86	53/99	../27	29
90	United Arab Emirates	..	..	..	90x	..	..	18/06	45/85	45/85	42/75	../.	24
91	Korea, Rep.	79	91	49	93	97	86	42/72	61/74	62/74	5/95	../.	..
92	Malaysia	79	96	66	..	..	..	91/99	54/91	61/90	../90	20/71	20
93	Mauritius	95	100	92	100	100	100	87/94	82/90	82/90	../84	1/94	7
94	Chile	89	100	21	97	..	..	100/97	97/99	96/99	93/98	../.	1
95	Uruguay	73	85	5	82	..	..	76/99	57/88	58/88	95/82	18/13	86
96	Yugoslavia	..	..	..	..	..	..	99/89x	90/91x	95/92x	95/93x	../.	..
97	Costa Rica	92	100	84	80x	100x	63x	81/92	83/95	85/95	71/90	../90	78
	Low U5MR countries (20 and under) Median	..	..	..	..	..	..	**95/91**	**85/90**	**90/94**	**70/85**	**../.**	..
98	Jamaica	71	95	46	90	..	..	../98	39/86	37/87	../74	50/..	15
99	Kuwait	100	100	..	100	..	..	../.	54/94	76/94	66/98	30/22	3
100	Poland	..	..	..	..	..	..	95/95	95/96	95/96	65/95	../.	..
101	Bulgaria	..	..	..	..	..	..	97/99x	97/99x	98/99x	98/99x	98/..	..
102	Trinidad and Tobago	98x	100x	95x	99	..	..	../.	52/82	55/87	../70	../.	60
103	Hungary	..	..	..	..	..	..	99/99	99/99	98/99	99/99	../.	..
104	Portugal	..	..	..	..	..	..	74/99	75/92	16/92	70/100	../.	..
105	Cuba	..	..	..	..	..	..	97/98	67/92	82/94	49/94	../88	75
106	Czechoslovakia	..	..	..	..	..	..	95/99	95/99	95/99	95/91	../.	..
107	New Zealand	97	100	82	..	..	..	../10x	72/69x	../75x	../67x	../.	..
108	Israel	..	..	..	..	..	..	70/..	84/87x	91/93x	69/86x	../.	..
109	Greece	..	..	..	..	..	..	95/..	95/83x	95/98x	../82x	../.	..
110	USA	..	..	..	..	..	..	../.	../97x	../97x	96/98x	../.	..
111	Italy	..	..	..	..	..	..	../.	../85x	../85	../50	../.	..
112	Norway	..	..	..	..	..	..	../.	../87	../84	../84	../.	..
113	Australia	..	..	..	..	..	..	../.	../93	../95	../85	../.	..
114	Spain	..	..	..	..	..	..	../.	../73x	../73x	../84x	../.	..
115	Belgium	..	..	..	..	..	..	../.	95/80	99/95	50/75	../.	..
116	Austria	..	..	..	..	..	..	90/90x	90/90x	90/90x	90/60x	../.	..
117	United Kingdom	..	..	..	..	..	..	../75	44/75	71/87	52/80	../.	..
118	Singapore	100	100	..	100	100	..	83/99	87/85	88/85	57/87	../.	..
119	France	..	..	..	..	..	..	80/80	79/95	80/95	../60	../.	..
120	Switzerland	..	..	..	..	..	..	../.	../90	../98	../90	../.	..
121	Denmark	..	..	..	..	..	..	95/..	85/99	97/100	../80	../.	..
122	Ireland	..	..	..	..	..	..	../80	36/77	76/72	../68	../.	..
123	Germany	..	..	..	..	..	..	54/84	58/95	83/95	50/60	../.	..
124	Canada	..	..	..	..	..	..	../.	../85x	../85x	../85x	../.	..
125	Netherlands	..	..	..	..	..	..	../.	97/94	97/94	93/93	../.	..
126	Hong Kong	100	100	96	99x	..	..	99/99	84/88	94/96	../41	../.	..
127	Finland	..	..	..	..	..	..	90/91	92/90	90/90	70/95	../.	..
128	Sweden	..	..	..	..	..	..	../14x	99/99x	99/98x	56/94x	../.	..
129	Japan	..	..	..	..	..	..	85/85	../87	../93	../77	../.	..

TABLE 4: EDUCATION

| | | Adult literacy rate | | | | No. of sets per 1000 population 1988 | | Primary school enrolment ratio | | | | | | % of grade 1 enrolment reaching final grade of primary school 1985-87 | Secondary school enrolment ratio 1986-89 (gross) | |
| | | 1970 | | 1990 | | | | 1960 (gross) | | 1986-89 (gross) | | 1986-89 (net) | | | | |
		male	female	male	female	radio	television	male	female	male	female	male	female		male	female
	Very high U5MR countries (over 140) Median	**27**	**8**	**49**	**24**	**93**	**6**	**35**	**16**	**70**	**50**	**52**	**38**	**50**	**19**	**9**
1	Mozambique	29	14	45	21	39	1	60	36	76	59	49	41	34	7	4
2	Afghanistan	13	2	44	14	102	8	15	2	33	17	..	..	78	10	7
3	Angola	16	7	56	29	50	6	..	..	101	85	..	..	24	17	9
4	Mali	11	4	41	24	38	..	14	6	29	17	23	14	40	9	4
5	Sierra Leone	18	8	31	11	218	9	30	..	65	40	..	..	..	23	11
6	Malawi	42	18	..	..	242	..	..	45	79	65	56	47	31	5	3
7	Guinea-Bissau	13	6	50	24	38	..	..	..	69	37	52	29	19	9	3
8	Guinea	21	7	35	13	34	3	44	16	42	19	31	15	43	13	4
9	Burkina Faso	13	3	28	9	25	5	12	5	41	24	34	20	68	8	4
10	Niger	6	2	40	17	63	4	7	3	38	21	..	..	75	8	3
11	Ethiopia	8	..	..	..	193	2	11	3	44	28	31	22	50	18	12
12	Chad	20	2	42	18	235	1	29	4	73	29	52	23	78	10	2
13	Somalia	5	1	27x	9x	40	0	13	13	20	10	14	8	33*	..	..
14	Mauritania	..	..	47	21	143	1	13	3	61	43	..	..	78	23	10
15	Liberia	27	8	50	29	225	18	45	18	43	24	..	..	..	..	..
16	Rwanda	43	21	64	37	57	..	..	..	67	64	63	63	46	7	5
17	Cambodia	..	..	48	22	107	8	..	..	..	..	..	..	50*	45	20
18	Burundi	29	10	61	40	56	0	27	9	68	50	52	37	87	6	3
19	Bhutan	..	..	51	25	15	..	5	..	31	20	..	..	..	7	2
20	Nepal	23	3	38	13	33	2	19	1	112	57	84	35	27*	35	17
21	Yemen	14	3	47y	21y	44	12	..	..	132	39	..	..	31y	42	7
22	Senegal	18	5	52	25	111	34	36	..	70	49	59	41	85	19	10
23	Bangladesh	36	12	47	22	41	4	66	26	76	64	67	44	20	24	11
24	Madagascar	56	43	88	73	196	6	58	45	99	95	67	65	48*	23	19
25	Sudan	28	6	43	12	233	53	35	14	58x	41x	23x	17x	76	23	17
26	Tanzania	48	18	93y	88y	20	1	33	18	67	66	50	51	71	5	3
27	Central African Rep.	26	6	52	25	62	3	53	12	83	51	59	39	56	17	6
28	Namibia	..	..	..	..	125	11	..	..	..	..	..	..	..	..	..
29	Nigeria	35	14	62	40	164	6	46	27	68	63	..	..	63*	28	18
30	Gabon	43	22	74	49	135	23	..	..	..	..	..	..	44	..	..
31	Uganda	52	30	62	35	99	6	..	32	76	63	43	38	76	16	9
32	Bolivia	68	46	85	71	574	77	78	50	97	85	88	78	60	40	35
33	Pakistan	30	11	47	21	86	13	46	13	51	28	..	..	49y	26	11
34	Laos	37	28	..	..	124	3	34	16	122	98	..	..	38*	23	22
35	Cameroon	47	19	66	43	126	12	87	43	119	102	85	74	70	32	21
36	Benin	23	8	32	16	76	4	38	15	83	43	66	34	36	23	9
37	Togo	27	7	56	31	179	6	63	24	124	78	87	59	52	36	12
38	India	47	20	62	34	78	7x	80	40	114	83	..	..	40*	50	29
	High U5MR countries (71-140) Median	**55**	**37**	**76**	**60**	**164**	**55**	**68**	**52**	**100**	**92**	**84**	**80**	**67**	**35**	**35**
39	Ghana	43	18	70	51	294	13	52	25	81	66	..	..	..	49	30
40	Côte d'Ivoire	26	10	67	40	128	54	68	24	82	58	..	..	73	26	12
41	Haiti	26x	17x	59	47	40	4	50	42	86	80	44	42	32	20	17
42	Zaire	61	22	84	61	99	1	88	32	86	65	..	..	60	32	14
43	Lesotho	49	74	..	..	68	1	63	102	101	123	..	..	52	20	30
44	Zambia	66	37	81	65	74	15	51	34	102	92	..	..	80	..	..
45	Peru	81	60	92	79	241	85	95	71	125	120	..	..	70	68	61
46	Libyan Arab Jamahiriya	60	13	75	50	223	70	92	24	..	..	..	..	82	..	..
47	Morocco	34	10	61	38	207	55x	67	27	80	53	65	46	67	43	30
48	Congo	50	19	70	44	122	3	103	53	..	..	..	..	71	37*	14*
49	Kenya	44	19	80	59	91	6	64	30	95	91	..	..	51	27	19
50	Algeria	39	11	70	46	229	71	55	37	105	87	97	81	90	61	53
51	Indonesia	66	42	84	62	146	41	86	58	121	117	100	97	80	53	43
52	Guatemala	51	37	63	47	63	37	50	39	82	70	..	..	36	21	19
53	Saudi Arabia	15	2	73	48	280	269	22	..	78	65	64	48	90	52	35
54	South Africa	..	..	..	..	323	98	94	85	..	..	..	..	..	..	..
55	Myanmar	85	57	89	72	79	2	61	52	106	100	..	..	33*	25	23
56	El Salvador	61	53	76	70	402	84	..	..	79	81	71	62	31	27	31
57	Zimbabwe	63	47	74	60	85	22	..	..	130	126	100	100	74	49	42
58	Iraq	50	18	70	49	200	68	94	36	104	87	90	82	73	60	37
59	Egypt	50	20	63	34	312	84	80	52	100	79	..	..	95	79	58
60	Botswana	37	44	84	65	134	7	35	48	114	120	94	100	89	31	36
61	Turkey	69	34	90	71	161	172	90	58	121	113	..	..	97	57	34
62	Mongolia	87	74	..	..	130	32	79	78	100	103	..	..	..	88	96
63	Honduras	55	50	76	71	383	68	68	67	104	108	89	94	43	28	36

Note: nations are listed in descending order of their 1990 under five mortality rates (see table 1).

| | | Adult literacy rate | | | | No. of sets per 1000 population 1988 | | Primary school enrolment ratio | | | | | | % of grade 1 enrolment reaching final grade of primary school 1985-87 | Secondary school enrolment ratio 1986-89 (gross) | |
| | | 1970 | | 1990 | | | | 1960 (gross) | | 1986-89 (gross) | | 1986-89 (net) | | | | |
		male	female	male	female	radio	television	male	female	male	female	male	female		male	female
64	Ecuador	75	68	88	84	293	81	87	79	118	116	. .	. .	63	55	57
65	Brazil	69	63	83	80	371	194	97	93	. .	. .	. .	. .	22	32	42
66	Papua New Guinea	39	24	65	38	64	2	59	7	79	67	78	. .	62	16	10
67	Nicaragua	58	57	. .	. .	246	61	65	66	94	104	74	79	35	29	58
68	Dominican Rep.	69	65	85	82	166	81	99	98	99	103	. .	78	35	. .	. .
	Middle U5MR countries (21-70) Median	**83**	**74**	**90**	**86**	**241**	**110**	**100**	**92**	**106**	**104**	**96**	**89**	**87**	**57**	**58**
69	Philippines	84	81	90	90	135	37	98	93	109	111	97	94	75	66	71
70	Viet Nam	. .	. .	92	84	103	34	. .	. .	107	94	. .	. .	57*	44	41
71	Tunisia	44	17	74	56	180	69	88	43	121	105	100	89	72	46	38
72	Paraguay	85ˣ	75ˣ	92	88	166	24	105	90	106	102	91	84	50	30	29
73	Syria	60	20	78	51	244	59	89	39	115	104	100	94	89	69	47
74	Iran, Islamic Rep. of	40	17	65	43	237	53	56	27	123	109	99	89	87	57	44
75	Lebanon	79ˣ	58ˣ	88	73	773	302	105	99	105	95	. .	. .	. .	57	56
76	Jordan	64	29	89	70	238	70	94	59	98	99	88	88	96	80	78
77	Colombia	79	76	88	86	170	110	77	77	112	115	72	74	57	55	56
78	Mexico	78	69	90	85	241	124	82	77	118	115	. .	. .	69	54	53
79	Oman	. .	. .	. .	. .	649	740	. .	. .	105	95	85	77	92	46	34
80	Venezuela	79	71	87	90	428	147	100	100	. .	107	107	88	90	48	59
81	China	. .	. .	84	62	184	24	. .	. .	142	126	100	95	77*	50	37
82	Albania	. .	. .	. .	. .	168	83	102	86	100	99	. .	. .	. .	80	71
83	Argentina	94	92	96	95	666	217	98	99	107	114	. .	. .	. .	69	78
84	Korea, Dem.	. .	. .	. .	. .	111	12	. .	. .	100	100	. .	. .	99	100	100
85	Sri Lanka	85	69	93	84	191	32	100	90	108	105	100	100	94	63	74
86	Thailand	86	72	96	90	177	104	88	79	98	94	. .	. .	64*	32	28
87	Romania	96	91	. .	. .	291	174ˣ	101	95	. .	. .	. .	. .	. .	79	80
88	USSR	98	97	. .	. .	686	319	100	100	106	104	. .	. .	98	. .	. .
89	Panama	81	81	88	88	222	164	98	94	108	104	90	89	82	56	63
90	United Arab Emirates	24	7	58*	38*	321	107	. .	. .	104	104	93	89	88	55	68
91	Korea, Rep.	94	81	99	94	986	203	99	89	107	108	100	99	99	91	83
92	Malaysia	71	48	87	70	438	142	108	83	102	102	. .	. .	99	59	57
93	Mauritius	77	59	. .	. .	264ˣ	188ˣ	103	93	104	105	94	95	98	53	53
94	Chile	90	88	94	93	338	183	111	107	101	99	. .	. .	85	72	78
95	Uruguay	93ˣ	93ˣ	97	96	595	173	111	111	110	108	. .	. .	86	68	76
96	Yugoslavia	92	76	97	88	195ˣ	179ˣ	113	108	95	94	. .	. .	98	82	79
97	Costa Rica	88	87	93	93	259	80	97	95	100	97	85	85	76	40	43
	Low U5MR countries (20 and under) Median	**95**	**89**	**. .**	**. .**	**586**	**379**	**105**	**103**	**102**	**102**	**97**	**97**	**95**	**86**	**87**
98	Jamaica	96	97	98	99	401	110	92	93	102	105	96	99	82	62	68
99	Kuwait	65	42	77	67	329	262	131	102	94	91	. .	77	90	86	79
100	Poland	98	97	. .	. .	294ˣ	263ˣ	110	107	101	101	99	99	93	78	82
101	Bulgaria	94	89	. .	. .	221ˣ	189ˣ	94	92	105	103	. .	. .	86	75	76
102	Trinidad and Tobago	95	89	. .	. .	458	297	. .	. .	99	100	87	88	84	80	85
103	Hungary	98	98	. .	. .	590	404	103	100	97	97	94	96	92	69	70
104	Portugal	78	65	89	82	215	160ˣ	132	129	131	123	. .	. .	. .	47	56
105	Cuba	86	87	95	93	337	203	109	109	107	101	97	94	91	85	96
106	Czechoslovakia	. .	. .	. .	. .	274ˣ	395	93	93	95	96	. .	. .	93	27	49
107	New Zealand	. .	. .	. .	. .	917	372	110	106	107	106	100	100	. .	84	86
108	Israel	93	83	. .	. .	468	265	99	97	94	97	. .	. .	. .	79	87
109	Greece	93	76	98	89	415	175ˣ	104	101	106	106	91	92	99	89	80
110	USA	99	99	. .	. .	2120	812	. .	. .	101	100	97	97	. .	98	99
111	Italy	95	93	98	96	790	419	112	109	. .	. .	97	98	100	76	76
112	Norway	. .	. .	. .	. .	795	350ˣ	100	100	95	95	97	97	100	92	97
113	Australia	. .	. .	. .	. .	1273	484	103	103	106	105	97	98	. .	96	99
114	Spain	93	87	97	93	302	380	106	116	113	113	98	98	98	97	107
115	Belgium	99	99	. .	. .	466ˣ	320ˣ	111	108	99	100	82	83	78	99	100
116	Austria	. .	. .	. .	. .	627	487	106	104	102	101	. .	. .	95	78	81
117	United Kingdom	. .	. .	. .	. .	1146	435	92	92	105	106	97	97	. .	82	85
118	Singapore	92	55	. .	. .	307ˣ	360	121	113	110	107	100	100	95	70	71
119	France	99	98	. .	. .	895	399	144	143	114	113	100	100	94	89	96
120	Switzerland	. .	. .	. .	. .	401ˣ	408	118	118	. .	. .	. .	. .	99	. .	. .
121	Denmark	. .	. .	. .	. .	452ˣ	526	103	103	98	99	. .	. .	100	106	107
122	Ireland	. .	. .	. .	. .	581	260	107	112	100	100	. .	. .	. .	91	101
123	Germany	. .	. .	. .	. .	895	378ˣ	. .	. .	103	102	. .	. .	99	92	88
124	Canada	. .	. .	. .	. .	960	586	108	105	106	104	97	97	. .	104	104
125	Netherlands	. .	. .	. .	. .	912	478	105	104	114	116	85	88	94	105	103
126	Hong Kong	90ˣ	64ˣ	. .	. .	634	247	93	79	106	105	. .	95	98ˣ	71	76
127	Finland	. .	. .	. .	. .	997	486	100	95	102	101	. .	. .	98	98	114
128	Sweden	. .	. .	. .	. .	875	395ˣ	95	96	100	100	. .	. .	100	90	92
129	Japan	99	99	. .	. .	863	589	103	102	102	102	100	100	100	95	97

TABLE 5: DEMOGRAPHIC INDICATORS

#		Population (millions) 1990		Population annual growth rate (%)		Crude death rate		Crude birth rate		Life expectancy		Total fertility rate 1990	% population urbanized 1990	Average annual growth rate of urban population (%)	
		under 16	under 5	1965-80	1980-90	1960	1990	1960	1990	1960	1990	1990	1990	1965-80	1980-90
	Very high U5MR countries (over 140) Median	**655T**	**241T**	**2.5**	**2.8**	**26**	**16**	**48**	**47**	**39**	**50**	**6.6**	**27**	**5.4**	**5.6**
1	Mozambique	7.2	2.8	2.5	2.6	26	18	47	45	37	48	6.3	27	11.8	9.7
2	Afghanistan	7.3	3.0	2.4	0.3	30	23	52	51	33	43	6.9	18	6.0	1.8
3	Angola	4.7	1.8	2.8	2.6	31	19	50	47	33	46	6.4	28	6.4	5.6
4	Mali	4.5	1.8	2.1	2.9	29	20	52	51	35	45	7.1	19	4.9	4.0
5	Sierra Leone	1.9	0.8	2.0	2.4	33	23	48	48	32	42	6.5	32	4.3	5.1
6	Malawi	4.4	1.8	2.9	3.5	28	20	54	56	38	48	7.6	12	7.8	6.0
7	Guinea-Bissau	0.4	0.2	1.2	1.9	29	22	40	43	34	43	5.8	20	1.7	3.5
8	Guinea	2.8	1.1	1.9	2.5	31	21	53	51	34	44	7.0	26	6.6	5.5
9	Burkina Faso	4.2	1.6	2.0	2.6	28	18	52	47	36	48	6.5	9	3.4	5.1
10	Niger	3.9	1.5	2.7	3.2	29	20	53	52	35	46	7.1	19	6.9	7.1
11	Ethiopia	23.5	9.3	2.7	2.4	28	20	51	49	36	46	6.8	13	6.6	4.5
12	Chad	2.6	1.0	2.0	2.4	30	19	46	44	35	47	5.8	30	9.2	6.2
13	Somalia	3.7	1.4	2.7	3.4	28	19	49	49	36	46	6.6	36	6.1	5.7
14	Mauritania	0.9	0.4	2.3	2.7	28	18	48	46	35	47	6.5	47	12.4	7.4
15	Liberia	1.2	0.5	3.0	3.2	25	15	50	47	41	54	6.8	46	6.2	5.9
16	Rwanda	3.7	1.5	3.3	3.4	22	16	50	51	42	50	8.1	8	6.3	7.7
17	Cambodia	3.0	1.4	0.3	2.5	21	16	45	39	42	50	4.6	12	1.9	3.8
18	Burundi	2.6	1.0	1.9	2.8	23	17	46	47	41	49	6.8	6	1.8	5.4
19	Bhutan	0.6	0.2	1.6	2.0	25	16	43	38	38	49	5.5	5	3.7	5.0
20	Nepal	8.5	3.1	2.4	2.5	26	14	46	38	38	52	5.7	10	5.1	7.0
21	Yemen	6.1	2.4	2.3	3.5	28	15	53	52	36	51	7.7	29	6.4	7.1
22	Senegal	3.5	1.3	2.5	2.8	27	17	50	45	37	48	6.3	38	4.1	3.7
23	Bangladesh	53.5	19.0	2.7	2.7	23	15	47	41	40	52	5.3	16	8.0	6.5
24	Madagascar	5.7	2.2	2.5	3.1	24	13	48	45	41	55	6.6	24	5.7	5.8
25	Sudan	11.9	4.5	3.0	3.0	25	15	47	44	39	51	6.4	22	5.1	4.1
26	Tanzania	14.0	5.6	3.3	3.7	24	13	51	50	41	54	7.1	33	8.7	10.6
27	Central African Rep.	1.4	0.6	1.8	2.7	26	17	43	45	39	50	6.2	47	4.8	4.7
28	Namibia	0.9	0.3	1.0	3.1	23	11	46	43	42	58	5.9	28	1.9	5.1
29	Nigeria	53.8	21.1	2.5	3.2	25	15	52	48	40	52	6.8	35	4.8	5.9
30	Gabon	0.4	0.2	3.5	3.7	24	16	31	41	41	53	5.2	46	4.2	6.2
31	Uganda	9.7	3.9	2.9	3.6	21	15	50	52	43	52	7.3	10	4.1	5.4
32	Bolivia	3.4	1.3	2.5	2.7	22	13	46	42	43	55	5.9	51	2.9	4.2
33	Pakistan	58.4	23.0	3.1	3.6	24	12	49	44	43	58	6.2	32	4.3	4.9
34	Laos	1.9	0.7	0.6	2.6	23	16	45	45	40	50	6.7	19	4.8	5.8
35	Cameroon	5.8	2.3	2.7	3.1	25	14	44	47	39	54	6.9	41	8.1	5.8
36	Benin	2.3	0.9	2.7	2.9	33	19	47	49	35	47	7.1	38	10.2	4.7
37	Togo	1.7	0.6	3.0	3.0	26	13	48	45	39	54	6.6	26	7.2	6.2
38	India	329.0	114.4	2.3	2.1	21	11	43	32	44	59	4.2	27	3.6	3.7
	High U5MR countries (71-140) Median	**326T**	**114T**	**2.8**	**2.8**	**20**	**9**	**49**	**38**	**46**	**62**	**5.2**	**46**	**4.7**	**4.4**
39	Ghana	7.1	2.8	2.2	3.4	19	13	48	44	45	55	6.3	33	3.4	4.1
40	Côte d'Ivoire	6.0	2.4	4.2	3.8	25	14	53	50	39	53	7.4	40	8.7	5.3
41	Haiti	2.8	1.0	2.0	1.9	24	13	42	36	42	56	4.9	28	4.0	3.7
42	Zaire	17.2	6.6	2.8	3.0	23	14	47	46	41	53	6.1	39	7.2	4.5
43	Lesotho	0.8	0.3	2.3	2.8	24	12	43	41	42	57	5.8	20	14.6	6.8
44	Zambia	4.3	1.8	3.1	3.9	23	13	50	51	42	54	7.2	50	7.1	6.1
45	Peru	8.6	2.9	2.8	2.2	19	8	47	30	48	63	3.8	70	4.1	3.1
46	Libyan Arab Jamahiriya	2.2	0.8	4.6	4.0	19	9	49	44	47	62	6.8	70	9.7	6.2
47	Morocco	10.7	3.8	2.5	2.6	21	9	50	34	47	62	4.5	48	4.2	4.1
48	Congo	1.1	0.4	2.7	3.1	23	14	45	46	42	54	6.3	40	3.5	4.3
49	Kenya	12.6	4.7	3.6	3.7	23	11	53	47	45	60	6.9	24	9.0	7.5
50	Algeria	11.5	3.8	3.1	2.9	20	8	51	35	47	65	5.1	52	3.8	4.6
51	Indonesia	70.0	22.8	2.3	2.0	23	9	44	28	41	61	3.3	31	4.7	5.2
52	Guatemala	4.4	1.6	2.8	2.8	20	8	49	40	46	63	5.6	39	3.6	3.4
53	Saudi Arabia	6.7	2.5	4.6	4.1	23	7	49	42	44	65	7.1	77	8.5	5.6
54	South Africa	13.8	4.9	2.4	2.2	17	9	42	31	49	62	4.3	59	2.6	3.4
55	Myanmar	16.4	5.6	2.3	2.1	21	9	42	30	44	61	3.9	25	2.8	2.4
56	El Salvador	2.5	0.8	2.7	1.5	16	8	49	36	51	64	4.7	44	3.5	2.2
57	Zimbabwe	4.6	1.7	3.1	3.1	20	10	53	41	45	60	5.6	28	7.5	5.4
58	Iraq	9.2	3.4	3.4	3.5	20	7	49	42	49	65	6.1	71	5.3	4.3
59	Egypt	21.7	7.6	2.4	2.5	21	10	45	33	46	60	4.3	47	2.9	3.1
60	Botswana	0.7	0.3	3.5	3.7	21	11	52	46	46	60	6.7	28	15.4	9.7
61	Turkey	20.5	7.1	2.4	2.3	18	8	45	28	50	65	3.5	61	4.3	5.7
62	Mongolia	1.0	0.3	3.0	2.8	18	8	43	35	47	63	4.9	52	4.5	2.9
63	Honduras	2.4	0.9	3.2	3.4	19	8	51	39	46	65	5.2	44	5.5	5.3

Note: nations are listed in descending order of their 1990 under five mortality rates (see table 1).

		Population (millions) 1990		Population annual growth rate (%)		Crude death rate		Crude birth rate		Life expectancy		Total fertility rate 1990	% population urbanized 1990	Average annual growth rate of urban population (%)	
		under 16	under 5	1965-80	1980-90	1960	1990	1960	1990	1960	1990			1965-80	1980-90
64	Ecuador	4.4	1.5	3.1	2.6	15	7	46	32	53	66	4.1	56	5.1	4.4
65	Brazil	56.1	19.0	2.4	2.1	13	8	43	27	55	66	3.3	75	4.5	3.4
66	Papua New Guinea	1.7	0.6	2.3	2.3	23	11	44	34	41	55	5.0	16	8.4	4.2
67	Nicaragua	1.9	0.7	3.1	3.3	18	7	51	40	47	65	5.3	60	4.6	4.5
68	Dominican Rep.	2.9	1.0	2.7	2.3	16	7	50	30	52	67	3.5	60	5.3	4.1
	Middle U5MR countries (21-70) Median	**634T**	**214T**	**2.5**	**2.0**	**13**	**6**	**43**	**26**	**57**	**70**	**3.0**	**54**	**4.0**	**3.2**
69	Philippines	26.4	9.2	2.9	2.6	15	7	46	32	53	64	4.1	43	4.0	3.9
70	Viet Nam	27.7	9.3	1.0	2.2	23	9	42	31	44	63	3.9	22	4.1	3.4
71	Tunisia	3.3	1.1	2.1	2.5	19	7	47	29	48	67	3.7	54	4.2	2.9
72	Paraguay	1.8	0.7	2.8	3.1	9	7	43	34	64	67	4.5	47	3.2	4.4
73	Syria	6.3	2.4	3.4	3.5	18	6	47	44	50	66	6.5	50	4.5	4.3
74	Iran, Islamic Rep. of	25.2	8.2	3.2	3.4	21	7	47	34	50	66	5.0	57	5.5	4.7
75	Lebanon	1.0	0.4	1.6	0.1	14	8	43	31	60	66	3.6	84	4.6	1.1
76	Jordan	1.9	0.7	2.6	3.2	23	6	50	39	47	67	5.8	68	5.3	4.4
77	Colombia	12.6	4.1	2.2	2.0	13	6	45	27	57	69	3.0	70	3.5	2.9
78	Mexico	35.1	11.6	3.1	2.3	12	6	46	28	57	70	3.3	73	4.5	3.2
79	Oman	0.7	0.3	3.6	4.2	28	7	51	44	40	66	7.1	11	8.1	7.9
80	Venezuela	8.0	2.7	3.5	2.7	10	5	45	30	60	70	3.6	90	4.5	3.6
81	China	324.3	112.3	2.2	1.3	19	7	37	21	47	70	2.4	33	2.6	6.7
82	Albania	1.1	0.4	2.5	1.9	10	6	41	23	62	72	2.9	35	3.4	2.4
83	Argentina	10.3	3.2	1.6	1.4	9	9	24	21	65	71	2.9	86	2.2	1.8
84	Korea, Dem.	6.7	2.4	2.7	1.8	13	5	42	24	54	70	2.5	60	4.6	2.3
85	Sri Lanka	6.0	1.8	1.8	1.5	9	6	36	22	62	71	2.6	21	2.3	1.4
86	Thailand	19.4	5.7	2.7	1.8	15	7	44	21	52	66	2.4	23	4.6	4.4
87	Romania	5.8	1.7	1.1	0.5	9	11	20	15	65	71	2.1	53	3.4	1.2
88	USSR	77.9	25.3	0.9	0.8	7	10	24	18	68	71	2.3	66	2.2	1.3
89	Panama	0.9	0.3	2.6	2.1	10	5	41	26	61	72	3.0	53	3.4	2.8
90	United Arab Emirates	0.5	0.2	16.1	4.5	19	4	46	22	53	70	4.6	78	18.9	4.1
91	Korea, Rep.	11.9	3.3	1.9	1.2	14	6	43	16	54	70	1.7	72	5.7	3.5
92	Malaysia	7.2	2.6	2.5	2.6	15	5	44	30	54	70	3.8	43	4.5	4.8
93	Mauritius	0.3	0.1	1.6	1.1	10	6	44	18	59	70	1.9	40	4.0	0.7
94	Chile	4.3	1.5	1.8	1.7	13	6	37	23	57	72	2.7	86	2.6	2.2
95	Uruguay	0.9	0.3	0.4	0.0	10	10	22	17	68	72	2.4	85	0.7	0.8
96	Yugoslavia	5.7	1.7	0.9	0.7	10	9	24	14	63	73	1.9	56	3.0	2.8
97	Costa Rica	1.1	0.4	2.6	2.8	10	4	47	27	62	75	3.1	47	3.7	3.7
	Low U5MR countries (20 and under) Median	**192T**	**59T**	**0.8**	**0.5**	**9**	**10**	**20**	**13**	**69**	**76**	**1.8**	**76**	**1.9**	**1.2**
98	Jamaica	0.9	0.3	1.5	1.4	10	6	39	23	63	73	2.5	52	3.4	2.5
99	Kuwait	0.8	0.3	7.0	3.9	10	2	44	27	60	73	3.7	96	8.2	4.5
100	Poland	10.3	3.0	0.8	0.8	8	10	24	16	67	72	2.2	62	1.8	1.4
101	Bulgaria	1.9	0.6	0.5	0.2	9	12	18	13	68	73	1.9	68	2.8	1.2
102	Trinidad and Tobago	0.5	0.2	1.3	1.7	9	6	38	25	64	72	2.8	69	5.0	3.6
103	Hungary	2.3	0.6	0.4	-0.1	10	13	16	12	68	71	1.8	61	1.8	1.2
104	Portugal	2.4	0.7	0.6	0.5	11	10	24	13	63	74	1.7	34	2.0	1.8
105	Cuba	2.6	0.9	1.5	0.9	9	7	31	18	64	75	1.9	75	2.7	1.9
106	Czechoslovakia	3.9	1.1	0.5	0.2	10	12	17	14	70	72	2.0	77	1.9	1.6
107	New Zealand	0.8	0.3	1.3	0.9	9	8	26	16	71	75	2.0	84	1.5	0.9
108	Israel	1.5	0.5	2.8	1.7	6	7	27	22	69	76	2.9	92	3.5	2.0
109	Greece	2.1	0.6	0.7	0.4	8	10	19	12	69	76	1.7	62	2.5	1.2
110	USA	56.9	18.3	1.0	0.9	9	9	23	15	70	76	1.8	75	1.2	1.1
111	Italy	10.4	2.8	0.6	0.1	10	10	18	10	69	76	1.4	69	1.0	0.4
112	Norway	0.9	0.3	0.6	0.3	9	11	18	13	73	77	1.7	75	5.0	0.9
113	Australia	4.0	1.2	1.8	1.4	9	8	22	15	71	77	1.8	85	0.2	1.3
114	Spain	8.5	2.3	1.0	0.4	9	9	21	13	69	77	1.6	78	2.4	1.2
115	Belgium	1.9	0.6	0.3	0.0	12	12	17	12	70	75	1.6	97	0.5	0.2
116	Austria	1.4	0.4	0.3	0.0	13	12	18	12	69	75	1.5	58	0.1	0.7
117	United Kingdom	11.6	3.8	0.2	0.2	12	12	17	14	71	76	1.8	89	0.5	0.2
118	Singapore	0.7	0.2	1.6	1.2	8	5	38	17	65	74	1.8	100	1.6	1.2
119	France	12.1	3.8	0.7	0.4	12	10	18	14	70	76	1.8	74	2.7	0.5
120	Switzerland	1.2	0.4	0.5	0.4	10	10	18	12	71	77	1.5	60	1.2	0.9
121	Denmark	0.9	0.3	0.5	0.0	9	11	17	11	72	76	1.5	87	1.1	0.4
122	Ireland	1.1	0.3	1.2	0.9	12	9	22	18	70	75	2.4	57	2.2	1.2
123	Germany	13.2	4.3	0.2	-0.1	12	12	17	11	70	75	1.5	85	0.9	0.2
124	Canada	5.9	1.8	1.3	1.0	8	8	26	14	71	77	1.7	77	1.5	1.2
125	Netherlands	2.9	0.9	0.9	0.6	8	9	21	13	73	77	1.6	89	1.5	0.6
126	Hong Kong	1.3	0.4	2.1	1.5	7	6	35	13	66	77	1.4	94	2.3	1.8
127	Finland	1.0	0.3	0.3	0.4	9	10	19	12	68	75	1.7	60	2.5	0.4
128	Sweden	1.6	0.5	0.5	0.2	10	12	15	13	73	77	1.9	84	1.0	0.3
129	Japan	24.7	6.8	1.2	0.6	8	7	18	11	68	79	1.7	77	2.1	0.7

TABLE 6: ECONOMIC INDICATORS

		GNP per capita (US $) 1989	GNP per capita average annual growth rate (%) 1965-80	GNP per capita average annual growth rate (%) 1980-89	Rate of inflation (%) 1980-89	% of population below absolute poverty level 1980-89 urban	% of population below absolute poverty level 1980-89 rural	% of central government expenditure allocated to (1986-90) health	education	defence	ODA inflow in millions US $ 1989	ODA inflow as % of recipient GNP 1989	Debt service as % of exports of goods and services 1970	Debt service as % of exports of goods and services 1989
	Very high U5MR countries (over 140) Median	**290**	**0.8**	**-1.1**	**8**	**36**	**61**	**5**	**12**	**16**	**320**	**13**	**4**	**14**
1	Mozambique	80	..	-6.0	35	50*	67*	5*	10*	35*	759	64	..	17
2	Afghanistan	280x	0.6	..	..	18x	36x				95	..	..	..
3	Angola	610	..	..	..	..	..	6*	15*	34*	140	2	..	..
4	Mali	270	2.1x	1.0	4	27x	48x	4*	17*	17*	470	22	1	10
5	Sierra Leone	220	0.7	-3.2	54	..	65x	6	13	3	99	12	11	6x
6	Malawi	180	3.2	-0.1	15	25	85	7	11	7	394	27	8	17
7	Guinea-Bissau	180	..	1.5	..	..	..	..	..	..	102	59	..	27
8	Guinea	430	1.3	..	..	..	..	3*	11*	29*	346	15	..	13
9	Burkina Faso	320	1.7	2.3	5	..	..	5	14	18	284	10	7	8
10	Niger	290	-2.5	-5.0	3	..	35x	..	..	..	296	13	4	9
11	Ethiopia	120	0.4	-1.1	2	60	65	..	..	..	702	12	11	34
12	Chad	190	-1.9	3.9	2	30x	56x	8*	8*	..	..	..	4	2
13	Somalia	170	-0.1	-1.3	43	40x	70x	1*	2*	38*	440	43	2	18
14	Mauritania	500	-0.1	-2.2	9	..	..	4*	23*	..	195	20	3	16
15	Liberia	450x	0.5	5.2x	..	..	23x	7	16	9	58	..	8	..
16	Rwanda	320	1.6	-1.9	4	30x	90x	5*	26*	..	238	11	1	14
17	Cambodia	..	..	..	..	..	..	..	..	..	25	..	..	..
18	Burundi	220	2.4	1.6	4	55x	85x	4*	16*	16*	198	17	2	30
19	Bhutan	190x	..	7.8x	..	..	..	5*	8*	..	40	..	..	..
20	Nepal	180	0.0	2.1	9	55x	61x	6	9	7	488	15	3	14
21	Yemen	650	..	..	..	..	..	..	..	..	338	5	..	17
22	Senegal	650	-0.5	0.0	7	..	..	..	..	..	652	14	3	21
23	Bangladesh	180	-0.3	0.7	11	86x	86x	10	11	10	1791	9	..	13
24	Madagascar	230	-0.4	-2.6	18	50x	50x	..	..	..	320	13	4	37
25	Sudan	420x	0.8	-1.8x	34x	..	85x	..	..	..	760	..	11	5
26	Tanzania	130	0.8	-1.6	26	..	..	6	8	16	918	30	5	13
27	Central African Rep.	390	0.8	-1.5	7	..	..	..	..	..	189	17	5	6
28	Namibia	1030	..	..	13	..	..	14*	18*	5*	44	..	..	..
29	Nigeria	250	4.2	-3.6	14	..	..	1	3	3	339	1	4	21
30	Gabon	2960	5.6	-2.6	-1	..	..	..	..	..	134	4	6	9
31	Uganda	250	-2.2	-1.0	108	..	..	2	15	26	397	9	3	45
32	Bolivia	620	1.7	-3.5	392	..	..	1	12	6	432	10	11	26
33	Pakistan	370	1.8	2.9	7	32x	29x	1	3	30	1119	3	24	16
34	Laos	180	..	0.0x	..	..	..	..	..	..	141	20	..	11
35	Cameroon	1000	2.4	0.7	7	15x	40x	4	13	8	470	4	3	7
36	Benin	380	-0.3	-1.8	8	..	..	..	..	..	247	14	2	5
37	Togo	390	1.7	-2.4	5	42x	..	5	20	11	182	13	3	12
38	India	340	1.5	3.2	8	29*	33*	2	3	19	1874	1	22	19x
	High U5MR countries (71-140) Median	**885**	**2.8**	**-0.7**	**12**	**31**	**51**	**7**	**15**	**11**	**227**	**4**	**7**	**17**
39	Ghana	390	-0.8	-0.8	44	59*	37*	9	26	3	543	10	6	22
40	Côte d'Ivoire	790	2.8	-3.0	3	30	26	4	21	4	409	4	7	10
41	Haiti	360	0.9	-0.7	7	65	80	..	..	..	198	8	59	6
42	Zaire	260	-1.3	-1.6	59	..	80x	4	6	14	637	7	4	4
43	Lesotho	470	6.8	-0.5	13	50x	55x	7	16	10	118	14	5	3
44	Zambia	390	-1.2	-3.8	38	25	..	7	9	..	388	13	6	11
45	Peru	1010	0.8	-1.6	160	46*	83*	6	16	20	300	1	12	4
46	Libyan Arab Jamahiriya	5310	0.0	-9.9x	0	..	..	..	..	..	11	0	..	..
47	Morocco	880	2.7	1.3	7	28x	45x	3	17	15	443	2	9	26
48	Congo	940	2.7	0.1	0	..	..	..	..	..	91	4	12	23
49	Kenya	360	3.1	0.4	9	10x	55x	5*	19*	8*	967	11	6	19
50	Algeria	2230	4.2	0.0	5	20x	..	..	..	..	153	0	4	68
51	Indonesia	500	5.2	3.6	8	20*	16*	2	10	8	1830	2	7	27
52	Guatemala	910	3.0	-2.6	13	17*	51*	8*	13*	19*	256	3	7	16
53	Saudi Arabia	6020	4.0x	-5.9	-4	..	..	..	..	..	16	0	..	..
54	South Africa	2470	3.2	-0.8	14	..	..	..	..	..	..	..	..	..
55	Myanmar	220x	1.6	..	..	40x	40x	8	12	19	220	..	12	29
56	El Salvador	1070	1.5	-1.1	17	20	32	7	17	26	446	8	4	13
57	Zimbabwe	650	1.7	-0.8	11	..	..	8	23	16	266	4	2	20
58	Iraq	2340x	..	..	30x	..	..	..	..	..	5	..	..	..
59	Egypt	640	2.8	2.8x	11	34*	34*	3	12	20	1578	5	38	17
60	Botswana	1600	9.9	6.7x	12	40	55	6	18	8	162	8	1	4
61	Turkey	1370	3.6	3.0	41	..	..	2	13	10	122	0	22	28
62	Mongolia	780x	..	..	..	..	..	..	..	..	4	..	..	..
63	Honduras	900	1.1	-1.2	5	31*	70*	..	..	..	256	6	3	10

Note: nations are listed in descending order of their 1990 under five mortality rates (see table 1).

#	Country	GNP per capita (US $) 1989	GNP per capita average annual growth rate (%)		Rate of inflation (%) 1980-89	% of population below absolute poverty level 1980-89		% of central government expenditure allocated to (1986-90)			ODA inflow in millions US $ 1989	ODA inflow as % of recipient GNP 1989	Debt service as % of exports of goods and services	
			1965-80	1980-89		urban	rural	health	education	defence			1970	1989
64	Ecuador	1020	5.4	-0.5	34	40	65	7	25	12	162	2	9	29
65	Brazil	2540	6.3	0.9	228	..	..	6	3	3	189	0	13	19
66	Papua New Guinea	890	..	-0.7	6	10x	75x	9	15	4	334	10	1	16
67	Nicaragua	830x	-0.7	-4.7x	87x	21x	19x	11*	9*	50*	227	..	11	..
68	Dominican Rep.	790	3.8	-0.1	19	45x	43x	8*	10*	5*	141	3	4	7
	Middle U5MR countries (21-70) Median	**1775**	**3.7**	**-0.2**	**14**	**18**	**20**	**5**	**14**	**8**	**91**	**0**	**11**	**15**
69	Philippines	710	3.2	-1.8	15	52*	64*	4	17	13	831	2	8	20
70	Viet Nam	240x	..	..	..	..	..	..	..	..	138	..	..	..
71	Tunisia	1260	4.7	0.6	8	20x	15x	6	15	6	247	2	20	21
72	Paraguay	1030	4.1	-1.5	23	19x	50x	3	12	12	91	2	12	10
73	Syria	980	5.1	-2.1	15	..	..	2	10	40	139	1	11	19x
74	Iran, Islamic Rep. of	3200	2.9	..	14	..	..	6	20	14	89	..	..	..
75	Lebanon	2150x	..	..	..	..	..	..	..	..	132	..	..	..
76	Jordan	1640	5.8x	-3.0	2x	14x	17x	4	14	30	280	5	4	15
77	Colombia	1200	3.7	0.9	24	32*	70*	..	..	..	62	0	12	38
78	Mexico	2010	3.6	-1.5	73	..	..	1	7	1	97	0	24	26
79	Oman	5220	9.0	5.3	-7	..	..	5	11	38	4	0	..	..
80	Venezuela	2450	2.3	-2.3	16	..	..	10	20	6	21	0	3	20
81	China	350	4.1	8.2	6	..	13*	..	..	8*	2227	1	..	8
82	Albania	..	..	..	..	..	..	..	..	..	9	..	..	..
83	Argentina	2160	1.7	-1.6	335	..	..	2	6	7	215	0	22	23
84	Korea, Dem.	970x	..	..	..	..	..	6	11	7	50	..	..	..
85	Sri Lanka	430	2.8	2.4	11	..	..	6	11	7	558	8	11	13
86	Thailand	1220	4.4	4.5	3	10*	25*	6	19	19	697	1	3	8
87	Romania	1620x	..	..	..	..	..	1	2	5	..	..	..	24x
88	USSR	4550x	..	..	..	..	..	..	..	..	..	..	..	..
89	Panama	1760	2.8	-2.1	3	21x	30x	20	19	8	17	0	8	0
90	United Arab Emirates	18430	..	8.2	1	..	..	7	14	44	-6	0	..	..
91	Korea, Rep.	4400	7.3	8.8	5	18x	11x	2	19	27	-9	0	20	7
92	Malaysia	2160	4.7	1.9	2	13	38	5*	..	..	139	0	4	12
93	Mauritius	1990	3.7	5.3	9	12x	12x	9	14	1	57	3	3	6
94	Chile	1770	0.0	1.0	21	12*	20*	4*	12*	..	61	0	19	15x
95	Uruguay	2020	2.5	-0.8	59	22*	..	4	9	8	38	0	22	20
96	Yugoslavia	2920	5.2	-0.7	97	..	..	..	..	55	43	0	10	8
97	Costa Rica	1780	3.3	0.4	25	8*	20*	17*	13*	3*	224	5	10	15
	Low U5MR (20 and under) Median	**14485**	**3.3**	**1.9**	**6**	**..**	**..**	**11**	**9**	**7**	**..**	**..**	**..**	**..**
98	Jamaica	1260	-0.1	-1.7	19	..	80	7*	11*	8*	258	9	3	16
00	Kuwait	16150	0.6x	-2.1	-3	..	..	8	14	14	4	0	..	..
100	Poland	1790	..	1.8	38	..	..	..	..	..	..	..	..	9
101	Bulgaria	2320	..	..	1	..	..	..	..	..	..	..	..	..
102	Trinidad and Tobago	3230	3.1	-7.3	6	..	39x	..	..	..	6	0	5	11
103	Hungary	2590	5.1	1.4	8	..	..	2	2	5	..	..	..	23x
104	Portugal	4250	4.6	2.1	19	..	..	..	..	..	79	0	7	17
105	Cuba	1170x	..	..	..	..	..	23*	10*	..	27	..	..	..
106	Czechoslovakia	3450	..	..	2	..	..	..	..	..	..	..	..	..
107	New Zealand	12070	1.7	0.9	11	..	..	12	11	5	..	..	..	..
108	Israel	9790	3.7	1.4	117	..	..	4	10	27	1192	3	3	..
109	Greece	5350	4.8	0.6	18	..	..	..	..	..	33	0	9	26x
110	USA	20910	1.8	2.2	4	..	..	13	2	25	..	..	..	..
111	Italy	15120	3.2	2.1	10	..	..	10	8	3	..	..	..	..
112	Norway	22290	3.6	3.5	6	..	..	11	9	8	..	..	..	..
113	Australia	14360	2.2	1.8	8	..	..	10	7	9	..	..	..	..
114	Spain	9330	4.1	2.4	9	..	..	13	6	6	..	..	..	..
115	Belgium	16220	3.6	1.7	5	..	..	2	13	5	..	..	..	..
116	Austria	17300	4.0	1.9	4	..	..	13	9	3	..	..	..	..
117	United Kingdom	14610	2.0	2.9	6	..	..	13	2	13	..	..	..	..
118	Singapore	10450	8.3	5.7	2	..	..	4	19	21	95	0	1	..
119	France	17820	3.7	1.6	7	..	..	21	8	6	..	..	..	..
120	Switzerland	29880	1.5	1.8	4	..	..	13	3	10	..	..	..	..
121	Denmark	20450	2.2	2.2	6	..	..	1	9	5	..	..	..	..
122	Ireland	8710	2.8	0.8	8	..	..	13	11	3	..	..	..	..
123	Germany	20440x	3.0x	2.1x	3x	..	..	..	..	..	..	..	..	..
124	Canada	19030	3.3	2.6	5	..	..	6	3	7	..	..	..	..
125	Netherlands	15920	2.7	1.3	2	..	..	11	12	5	..	..	..	..
126	Hong Kong	10350	6.2	5.7	7	..	..	8*	17*	..	23	0	..	..
127	Finland	22120	3.6	2.9	7	..	..	11	14	5	..	..	..	..
128	Sweden	21570	2.0	2.0	7	..	..	1	9	7	..	..	..	..
129	Japan	23810	5.1	3.5	1	..	..	..	..	..	..	..	..	..

TABLE 7: WOMEN

		Life expectancy females as a percentage of males 1990	Adult literacy rate females as a percentage of males 1990	Enrolment ratios females as a percentage of males 1986-89		Contraceptive prevalence (%) 1980-90	Pregnant women immunized against Tetanus 1989-90	% of births attended by trained health personnel 1983-90	Maternal mortality rate 1980-90
				Primary-school	Secondary-school				
	Very high U5MR countries (over 140) Median	**106.3**	**48**	**65**	**50**	**5**	**44**	**28**	**570**
1	Mozambique	106.5	47	78	57	4	25	28	300
2	Afghanistan	102.4	32	52	70	2ˣ	3	9*	640*
3	Angola	106.8	52	84	53	1ˣ	26	15	. .
4	Mali	109.3	59	59	44	3	31	27	2000
5	Sierra Leone	110.0	35	62	48	4*	77	25	450
6	Malawi	104.3	. .	82	60	7	82	45	170
7	Guinea-Bissau	107.3	48	54	33	. .	44	. .	700ˣ
8	Guinea	102.3	37	45	31	1ˣ	10	25	800*
9	Burkina Faso	106.4	32	59	50	1	76	30	810
10	Niger	106.8	43	55	38	1ˣ	44	47	700
11	Ethiopia	106.8	. .	64	67	2	43	14	. .
12	Chad	106.7	43	40	20	1ˣ	42	24ˣ	960*
13	Somalia	109.1	33ˣ	50	. .	. .	5	2	1100
14	Mauritania	108.9	45	70	43	1	40	20	. .
15	Liberia	105.7	58	56	. .	6	20ˣ	87	. .
16	Rwanda	106.3	58	96	71	10	87	22	210ˣ
17	Cambodia	106.3	46	. .	44	. .	. .	47*	500
18	Burundi	106.4	66	74	50	7	56	19	. .
19	Bhutan	96.0	49	65	29	. .	63	7	1310
20	Nepal	98.1	34	51	49	14	28	6	830
21	Yemen	102.9	45ʸ	30	17	. .	8	12	. .
22	Senegal	104.3	48	70	53	5	45	41	600
23	Bangladesh	100.0	47	84	46	25	74	5	600
24	Madagascar	105.7	83	96	83	. .	60	62	570
25	Sudan	104.0	28	71ˣ	74	9	14	60	550
26	Tanzania	107.7	95ʸ	99	60	1ˣ	42	60	340ˣ
27	Central African Rep.	110.6	48	61	35	. .	87	66	600
28	Namibia	105.4	. .	. .	. .	. .	50	. .	370ʸ
29	Nigeria	106.0	65	93	64	6	58	40ˣ	800
30	Gabon	105.9	66	. .	. .	. .	86	80	190
31	Uganda	108.0	56	83	56	5	31	38	300
32	Bolivia	109.6	84	88	88	30	20	42	600
33	Pakistan	100.0	45	55	42	8	87	40*	500
34	Laos	106.3	. .	80	96	. .	10	. .	. .
35	Cameroon	105.8	65	86	66	2ˣ	63	10	430
36	Benin	108.9	50	52	39	9	83	45	160ˣ
37	Togo	107.7	55	63	33	12	81	15*	420*
38	India	100.0	55	73	58	34	77	33	460
	High U5MR countries (71-140) Median	**106.3**	**75**	**94**	**86**	**33**	**48**	**50**	**200**
39	Ghana	107.5	73	81	61	13	33	55*	1000
40	Côte d'Ivoire	105.8	60	71	46	3	63	20	. .
41	Haiti	105.6	80	93	85	7	23	40	340*
42	Zaire	107.8	73	76	44	1ˣ	29	. .	800*
43	Lesotho	117.0	. .	122	150	5ˣ	. .	40	. .
44	Zambia	105.7	80	90	. .	1ˣ	68	39*	150
45	Peru	106.6	86	96	90	46	9	78*	300
46	Libyan Arab Jamahiriya	106.7	67	. .	. .	. .	6	76	80ˣ
47	Morocco	106.7	62	66	70	36	64	29ˣ	300*
48	Congo	109.8	63	. .	38*	. .	60	. .	900*
49	Kenya	106.9	74	96	70	27	37	28	170ˣ
50	Algeria	103.1	66	83	87	7ˣ	27	15	140ˣ
51	Indonesia	105.0	74	97	81	48	41	49	450
52	Guatemala	108.2	75	85	90	23	48	34	200*
53	Saudi Arabia	104.8	66	83	67	. .	62	88*	. .
54	South Africa	110.2	. .	. .	. .	48	. .	. .	83ˣ
55	Myanmar	105.0	81	94	92	5	56	57	460
56	El Salvador	111.5	92	103	115	47	12	50	. .
57	Zimbabwe	105.2	81	97	86	43	60	60	. .
58	Iraq	103.1	70	84	62	. .	67	50*	120
59	Egypt	105.1	54	79	73	38	63	47	320
60	Botswana	110.5	77	105	116	33	62	78*	200*
61	Turkey	104.7	79	93	60	77*	15	77*	150
62	Mongolia	104.9	. .	103	109	. .	. .	99	140*
63	Honduras	106.3	93	104	129	35	51	66	220

Note: nations are listed in descending order of their 1990 under five mortality rates (see table 1).

84

		Life expectancy females as a percentage of males 1990	Adult literacy rate females as a percentage of males 1990	Enrolment ratios females as a percentage of males 1986-89		Contraceptive prevalence (%) 1980-90	Pregnant women immunized against Tetanus 1989-90	% of births attended by trained health personnel 1983-90	Maternal mortality rate 1980-90
				Primary-school	Secondary-school				
64	Ecuador	106.3	95	98	104	44	8	56*	170*
65	Brazil	107.9	96	. .	131	66	62	95	200
66	Papua New Guinea	103.7	58	85	63	4	70	20	900
67	Nicaragua	104.8	. .	111	200	27	25	41x	. .
68	Dominican Rep.	106.2	96	104	. .	50	24	90	. .
	Midddle U5MR countries (21-70) Median	**107.1**	**94**	**98**	**98**	**54**	**53**	**88**	**80**
69	Philippines	106.5	100	102	108	45	47	57	100
70	Viet Nam	108.3	91	88	93	20	18	95*	120
71	Tunisia	103.0	76	87	83	50	40	68	50*
72	Paraguay	106.2	96	96	97	45	58	30	300
73	Syria	106.3	65	90	68	20x	84	61	140
74	Iran, Islamic Rep. of	101.5	66	89	77	23x	47	70*	120
75	Lebanon	106.3	83	90	98	. .	. .	. .	. .
76	Jordan	106.2	79	101	98	26	23	83	48x
77	Colombia	109.1	98	103	102	65	40	71	200
78	Mexico	110.6	94	97	98	53	42	94	110*
79	Oman	106.3	. .	90	74	. .	97	60	. .
80	Venezuela	109.0	103	. .	123	49x	. .	69	. .
81	China	104.3	74	89	74	74	. .	94	95x
82	Albania	107.1	. .	99	89	. .	. .	99	. .
83	Argentina	108.8	99	107	113	74	. .	. .	140
84	Korea, Dem.	109.0	. .	100	100	. .	99	100	41
85	Sri Lanka	105.8	90	97	117	62	60	94	80
86	Thailand	106.3	94	96	88	66	79	71	. .
87	Romania	108.8	. .	. .	101	58x	. .	100x	150
88	USSR	113.6	. .	98	. .	. .	. .	. .	21
89	Panama	107.1	100	96	113	58	27	89	60
90	United Arab Emirates	107.2	88	100	124	. .	. .	99	. .
91	Korea, Rep.	109.0	95	101	91	77*	. .	89	26
92	Malaysia	105.9	80	100	97	51	71	82	59
93	Mauritius	107.5	. .	101	100	75	94	85	99
94	Chile	110.3	99	98	108	43x		98	67
95	Uruguay	110.1	99	98	112	. .	13	97x	36
96	Yugoslavia	108.8	91	99	96	55x	. .	86x	8
97	Costa Rica	105.5	100	97	108	70	90	97	36
	Low U5MR countries (20 and under) Median	**108.4**	**. .**	**100**	**103**	**73**	**. .**	**99**	**8**
98	Jamaica	105.6	101	103	110	52		90	120
99	Kuwait	105.6	87	97	92	. .	22	99	6
100	Poland	111.8	. .	100	105	75x	. .	100x	11
101	Bulgaria	108.6	. .	98	101	76x	. .	100	9
102	Trinidad and Tobago	107.2	. .	101	106	53	. .	98	110
103	Hungary	111.9	. .	100	101	73	. .	99x	15
104	Portugal	108.5	92	94	119	66x	. .	87x	10
105	Cuba	104.1	98	94	113	60	88	99	39
106	Czechoslovakia	111.8	. .	101	181	95x	. .	100	10
107	New Zealand	108.3	. .	99	102	70x	. .	99	13
108	Israel	105.4	. .	103	110	. .	. .	99	3
109	Greece	105.4	91	100	90	. .	. .	97x	5
110	USA	109.7	. .	99	101	68	. .	99	8
111	Italy	108.2	98	. .	100	78x	. .	. .	4
112	Norway	108.1	. .	100	105	71x	. .	. .	3
113	Australia	109.6	. .	99	103	67x	. .	99x	3
114	Spain	108.1	96	100	110	59	. .	96	5
115	Belgium	109.7	. .	101	101	81x	. .	100	3
116	Austria	109.9	. .	99	104	71x	. .	. .	8
117	United Kingdom	108.2	. .	101	104	83	. .	100x	8
118	Singapore	108.5	. .	97	101	74	. .	100*	10
119	France	111.1	. .	99	108	79x	. .	99x	9
120	Switzerland	109.5	. .	. .	. .	71x	. .	99x	5
121	Denmark	108.2	. .	101	101	. .	. .	100x	3
122	Ireland	106.9	. .	100	111	. .	. .	. .	2
123	Germany	109.4	. .	99	96	. .	. .	99x	. .
124	Canada	109.5	. .	98	100	73	. .	99	5
125	Netherlands	109.5	. .	102	98	76	. .	100x	10
126	Hong Kong	106.7	. .	99	107	72	. .	100*	6*
127	Finland	109.7	. .	99	116	80x	. .	100x	11
128	Sweden	106.7	. .	100	102	78	. .	100x	5
129	Japan	106.6	. .	100	102	64	. .	100	11

TABLE 8: BASIC INDICATORS ON LESS POPULOUS COUNTRIES

		Under 5 mortality rate		Infant mortality rate		Total population (thousands) 1990	Annual no. of births (thousands) 1990	Annual no. of under 5 deaths (thousands) 1990	GNP per capita (US $) 1989	Life expectancy at birth (years) 1990	Total adult literacy rate 1985-90	% of age group enrolled in primary school Total 1986-89	% of children immunized against measles 1989-90
		1960	1990	1960	1990								
1	Gambia	375	238	213	138	861	39.7	9.0	240	44	27	61	73
2	Equatorial Guinea	316	206	188	122	352	15.5	3.0	330	47	50	108x	88
3	Swaziland	226	167	152	113	789	37.2	6.0	900	57	55x	105	85
4	Djibouti	. .	164	186	117	409	18.9	3.0	1210x	48	12*	46	85
5	Comoros	279	151	165	94	551	26.2	4.0	460	55	48x	80	87
6	Vanuatu	. .	91	. .	69	159	6.0	1.0	860	65	53x	84y	66
7	Kiribati	. .	88	. .	58	66	2.0	0.2	700	56	96	100y	63
8	Maldives	. .	85	. .	61	215	8.4	. .	420	62	95*	87*	89
9	Guyana	126	71	100	52	796	20.4	1.0	340	64	92x	79	73
10	Samoa	. .	59	. .	46	169	5.0	0.3	700	66	98*	91y	82
11	Cape Verde	164	56	110	41	370	15.3	1.0	780	67	37x	110	79
12	Sao Tome and Principe	. .	55	. .	43	121	4.0	0.2	340	66	57x	. .	57
13	St.Christopher-Nevis	. .	44	. .	37	44	1.0	0.0	2860x	70	90*	100	99
14	Tuvalu	. .	. .	. .	34y	10	. .	. .	650x	. .	90*	. .	79
15	Suriname	95	38	70	31	422	11.2	0.4	1900	70	95	125	65
16	Grenada	. .	38	. .	31	85	2.5	0.1	1900	70	96x	88x	85
17	Solomon Islands	. .	. .	. .	30	321	12.2	. .	580	70	15*	65y	70
18	Montserrat	. .	36	. .	30	13	0.0	0.0	3330x	71	97x	100y	99
19	Qatar	239	36	145	29	368	10.8	0.4	15500	69	76	117	79
20	British Virgin Islands	. .	. .	. .	27	13	0.2	. .	2100x	69y	98x	. .	99
21	Fiji	97	31	71	26	765	19.6	1.0	1650	65	79x	129	84
22	Turks and Caicos Islands	. .	. .	. .	25	10	0.2	. .	780x	. .	98x	. .	81
23	Bahamas	. .	. .	. .	25	254	5.1	. .	11320	72	70x	. .	87
24	Belize	. .	29	. .	23*	188	7.0	0.2	1720	68	93*	90	81
25	Fed. States of Micronesia	. .	28	. .	23	99	3.5	0.1	. .	74	63x	101y	12
26	St. Vincent & the Grenadines	. .	27	. .	23	116	3.0	0.1	1200x	70	82*	95x	96
27	Palau	. .	. .	. .	23*	18	0.6*	. .	790y	74*	75	98y	98
28	Marshall Islands	. .	. .	. .	23*	40	1.3*	. .	. .	74*	76x	107*	25x
29	Tonga	. .	26	. .	22	95	3.0	0.1	910	67	78*	100y	63
30	Antigua	. .	24	. .	20	77	1.0	0.0	3880x	74	95*	100	89
31	Saint Lucia	. .	23	. .	19	151	4.0	0.1	1810	71	82x	95y	82
32	Seychelles	. .	21	. .	18	69	2.0	0.0	3010	70	88*	102y	89
33	Dominica	. .	20	. .	17	83	2.0	0.0	1670x	75	94x	100	88
34	Cook Islands	. .	. .	. .	15	18	0.4	. .	1550x	. .	75*	100	100
35	Bahrain	208	17	130	14	516	13.7	0.2	6360x	71	77	110	86
36	Malta	42	14	37	11	353	4.9	0.1	5830	73	88	108	86
37	Cyprus	36	13	30	11	701	12.4	0.2	7040	76	89x	104	76
38	Barbados	90	12	74	11	255	4.1	0.1	6350	75	98*	110x	87
39	Brunei Darussalam	. .	. .	. .	9	266	6.4	. .	20760x	74	78x	. .	99x
40	Luxembourg	41	8	33	7	373	4.4	0.1	24980	75	. .	. .	71x
41	Iceland	22	5	17	4	254	4.1	0.0	21070	78	. .	102	99

Note: nations are listed in descending order of their 1990 infant mortality rate where no under five mortality rate is available.

Measuring human development

An introduction to Table 9

If development in the 1990s is to assume a more human face then there arises a corresponding need for a means of measuring human as well as economic progress. From UNICEF's point of view, in particular, there is a need for an agreed method of measuring the level of child well-being and its rate of change.

The under five mortality rate (U5MR) is used in Table 9 (next page) as the principle indicator of such progress.

U5MR has several advantages. First, it measures an end result of the development process rather than an 'input' such as school enrolment level, per capita calorie availability, or the number of doctors per thousand population - all of which are means to an end.

Second, the U5MR is known to be the result of a wide variety of inputs: the nutritional health and the health knowledge of mothers; the level of immunization and ORT use; the availability of maternal and child health services (including pre-natal care); income and food availability in the family; the availability of clean water and safe sanitation; and the overall safety of the child's environment.

Third, U5MR is less susceptible than, say, per capita GNP to the fallacy of the average. This is because the natural scale does not allow the children of the rich to be one thousand times as likely to survive, even if the man-made scale does permit them to have one thousand times as much income. In other words, it is much more difficult for a wealthy minority to affect a nation's U5MR, and it therefore presents a more accurate, if far from perfect, picture of the health status of the majority of children (and of society as a whole).

For these reasons, the U5MR is chosen by UNICEF as its single most important indicator of the state of a nation's children. That is why the statistical annex lists the nations of the world not in ascending order of their per capita GNP but in descending order of their under five mortality rates.

Measuring the rate of progress

The speed of progress in reducing the U5MR can be measured by calculating its average annual reduction rate (AARR). Unlike the comparison of absolute changes, the AARR reflects the fact that the limits to U5MR are approached only with increasing difficulty. As lower levels of under five mortality are reached, for example, the same absolute reduction obviously represents a greater percentage of reduction. The AARR therefore shows a higher rate of progress for, say, a ten point reduction if that reduction happens at a lower level of under five mortality. (A fall in U5MR of 10 points from 100 to 90 represents a reduction of 10%, whereas the same 10-point fall from 20 to 10 represents a reduction of 50%).

When used in conjunction with GNP growth rates, the U5MR and its reduction rate can therefore give a picture of the progress being made by any country or region, and over any period of time, towards the satisfaction of some of the most essential of human needs.

As Table 9 shows, there is no fixed relationship between the annual reduction rate of the U5MR and the annual rate of growth in per capita GNP. Such comparisons help to throw the emphasis on to the policies, priorities, and other factors which determine the ratio between economic and social progress.

Finally, the table gives the total fertility rate for each country and its average annual rate of reduction. It will be seen that many of the nations which have achieved significant reductions in U5MR have also achieved significant reductions in fertility.

TABLE 9: THE RATE OF PROGRESS

		Under 5 mortality rate			average annual rate of reduction (%)			GNP per capita average annual growth rate (%)		Total fertility rate			average annual rate of reduction (%)	
		1960	1980	1990	1960-80	1980-90	required** 1990-2000	1965-80	1980-89	1960	1980	1990	1960-80	1980-90
	Very high U5MR countries (over 140) Median	**302**	**238**	**189**	**1.3**	**1.7**	**9.9**	**0.8**	**-1.1**	**6.7**	**6.6**	**6.6**	**-0.1**	**0.0**
1	Mozambique	331	268	297	1.1	-1.0	14.5	. .	-6.0	6.3	6.5	6.3	-0.2	0.3
2	Afghanistan	381	320	292	0.9	0.9	14.3	0.6	. .	6.9	7.1	6.9	-0.1	0.3
3	Angola	344	261	292	1.4	-1.1	14.3	. .	. .	6.4	6.4	6.4	0.0	0.0
4	Mali	369	325	284	0.6	1.3	14.0	2.1ˣ	1.0	7.1	7.1	7.1	0.0	0.0
5	Sierra Leone	385	300	257	1.2	1.5	13.0	0.7	-3.2	6.2	6.5	6.5	-0.2	0.0
6	Malawi	366	299	253	1.0	1.7	12.8	3.2	-0.1	6.9	7.6	7.6	-0.5	0.0
7	Guinea-Bissau	336	290	246	0.7	1.6	12.6	. .	1.5	5.1	5.7	5.8	-0.6	-0.2
8	Guinea	336	275	237	1.0	1.5	12.2	1.3	. .	7.0	7.0	7.0	0.0	0.0
9	Burkina Faso	363	266	228	1.6	1.5	11.8	1.7	2.3	6.7	6.5	6.5	0.2	0.0
10	Niger	321	259	221	1.1	1.6	11.5	-2.5	-5.0	7.1	7.1	7.1	0.0	0.0
11	Ethiopia	294	260	220	0.6	1.7	11.5	0.4	-1.1	6.7	6.8	6.8	-0.1	0.0
12	Chad	325	254	216	1.2	1.6	11.3	-1.9	3.9	6.0	5.9	5.8	0.1	0.2
13	Somalia	294	247	215	0.9	1.4	11.2	-0.1	-1.3	6.6	6.6	6.6	0.0	0.0
14	Mauritania	321	249	214	1.3	1.5	11.2	-0.1	-2.2	6.5	6.5	6.5	0.0	0.0
15	Liberia	310	245	205	1.2	1.8	10.7	0.5	5.2ˣ	6.6	6.8	6.8	-0.1	0.0
16	Rwanda	248	231	198	0.4	1.5	10.4	1.6	-1.9	7.5	8.5	8.1	-0.6	0.5
17	Cambodia	218	330	193	-2.1	5.4	10.1	. .	. .	6.3	4.6	4.6	1.6	0.0
18	Burundi	260	225	192	0.7	1.6	10.1	2.4	1.6	6.8	6.8	6.8	0.0	0.0
19	Bhutan	298	222	189	1.5	1.6	9.9	. .	7.8ˣ	6.0	5.6	5.5	0.3	0.2
20	Nepal	298	222	189	1.5	1.6	9.9	0.0	2.1	5.8	6.4	5.7	-0.5	1.2
21	Yemen	378	235	187	2.4	2.3	9.8	. .	. .	7.5	7.7	7.7	-0.1	0.0
22	Senegal	299	232	185	1.3	2.3	9.7	-0.5	0.0	7.0	6.9	6.3	0.1	0.9
23	Bangladesh	262	212	180	1.1	1.6	9.4	-0.3	0.7	6.7	6.4	5.3	0.2	1.9
24	Madagascar	364	216	176	2.6	2.0	9.2	-0.4	-2.6	6.6	6.6	6.6	0.0	0.0
25	Sudan	292	210	172	1.6	2.0	9.0	0.8	-1.8ˣ	6.7	6.6	6.4	0.1	0.3
26	Tanzania	249	202	170	1.0	1.7	8.9	0.8	-1.6	6.8	7.1	7.1	-0.2	0.0
27	Central African Rep.	308	213	169	1.8	2.3	8.8	0.8	-1.5	5.6	6.0	6.2	-0.3	-0.3
28	Namibia	263	202	167	1.3	1.9	8.7	. .	. .	6.0	6.1	5.9	-0.1	0.3
29	Nigeria	316	198	167	2.3	1.7	8.7	4.2	-3.6	6.8	6.9	6.8	-0.1	0.1
30	Gabon	287	194	164	2.0	1.7	8.5	5.6	-2.6	4.1	4.4	5.2	-0.4	-1.7
31	Uganda	223	186	164	0.9	1.3	8.5	-2.2	-1.0	6.9	7.2	7.3	-0.2	-0.1
32	Bolivia	282	207	160	1.5	2.6	8.3	1.7	-3.5	6.7	6.3	5.9	0.3	0.7
33	Pakistan	276	193	158	1.8	2.0	8.1	1.8	2.9	6.9	7.0	6.2	-0.1	1.2
34	Laos	233	190	152	1.0	2.2	7.8	. .	0.0ˣ	6.2	6.7	6.7	-0.4	0.0
35	Cameroon	275	175	148	2.3	1.7	7.5	2.4	0.7	5.8	6.7	6.9	-0.7	-0.3
36	Benin	310	176	147	2.8	1.8	7.4	-0.3	-1.8	6.9	7.1	7.1	-0.1	0.0
37	Togo	305	184	147	2.5	2.2	7.4	1.7	-2.4	6.6	6.6	6.6	0.0	0.0
38	India	282	181	142	2.2	2.4	7.1	1.5	3.2	5.9	4.8	4.2	1.0	1.3
	High U5MR countries (71-140) Median	**229**	**133**	**90**	**2.5**	**2.9**	**4.1**	**2.8**	**-0.7**	**6.9**	**6.0**	**5.2**	**0.6**	**1.3**
39	Ghana	224	166	140	1.5	1.7	6.9	-0.8	-0.8	6.9	6.5	6.3	0.3	0.3
40	Côte d'Ivoire	264	167	136	2.3	2.1	6.6	2.8	-3.0	7.2	7.4	7.4	-0.1	0.0
41	Haiti	270	163	130	2.5	2.3	6.2	0.9	-0.7	6.3	5.3	4.9	0.9	0.8
42	Zaire	269	163	130	2.5	2.3	6.2	-1.3	-1.6	6.0	6.1	6.1	-0.1	0.0
43	Lesotho	208	161	129	1.3	2.2	6.1	6.8	-0.5	5.8	5.8	5.8	0.0	0.0
44	Zambia	228	146	122	2.2	1.8	5.6	-1.2	-3.8	6.6	7.2	7.2	-0.4	0.0
45	Peru	233	144	116	2.4	2.2	5.1	0.8	-1.6	6.9	5.0	3.8	1.6	2.7
46	Libyan Arab Jamahiriya	269	150	112	2.9	2.9	4.7	0.0	-9.9ˣ	7.1	7.3	6.8	-0.1	0.7
47	Morocco	265	153	112	2.7	3.1	4.7	2.7	1.3	7.2	5.7	4.5	1.2	2.4
48	Congo	241	132	110	3.0	1.8	4.5	2.7	0.1	5.9	6.3	6.3	-0.3	0.0
49	Kenya	208	133	108	2.2	2.1	4.3	3.1	0.4	8.0	8.0	6.9	0.0	1.5
50	Algeria	270	147	98	3.0	4.1	4.1	4.2	0.0	7.3	6.8	5.1	0.4	2.9
51	Indonesia	225	138	97	2.4	3.5	4.1	5.2	3.6	5.5	4.4	3.3	1.1	2.9
52	Guatemala	230	130	94	2.9	3.2	4.1	3.0	-2.6	6.9	6.3	5.6	0.5	1.2
53	Saudi Arabia	292	131	91	4.0	3.6	4.1	4.0ˣ	-5.9	7.2	7.3	7.1	-0.1	0.3
54	South Africa	192	120	88	2.4	3.1	4.1	3.2	-0.8	6.5	4.9	4.3	1.4	1.3
55	Myanmar	230	118	88	3.3	2.9	4.1	1.6	. .	6.0	4.8	3.9	1.1	2.1
56	El Salvador	207	122	87	2.6	3.4	4.1	1.5	-1.1	6.8	5.5	4.7	1.1	1.6
57	Zimbabwe	181	116	87	2.2	2.9	4.1	1.7	-0.8	7.5	6.4	5.6	0.8	1.3
58	Iraq	222	110	86	3.5	2.5	4.1	. .	. .	7.2	6.8	6.1	0.3	1.1
59	Egypt	301	172	85	2.8	7.0	4.1	2.8	2.8ˣ	7.0	5.2	4.3	1.5	1.9
60	Botswana	173	110	85	2.3	2.6	4.1	9.9	6.7ˣ	6.8	7.1	6.7	-0.2	0.6
61	Turkey	258	139	85	3.1	4.9	4.1	3.6	3.0	6.3	4.3	3.5	1.9	2.1
62	Mongolia	185	112	84	2.5	2.9	4.1	. .	. .	6.0	5.4	4.9	0.5	1.0
63	Honduras	232	141	84	2.5	5.2	4.1	1.1	-1.2	7.3	6.4	5.2	0.7	2.1

** The average annual reduction rate required to achieve an under five mortality rate in all countries of 70 per 1000 live births or of two-thirds the 1990 rate, whichever is less.

Note: nations are listed in descending order of their 1990 under five mortality rates (see table 1).

		Under 5 mortality rate			average annual rate of reduction (%)			GNP per capita average annual growth rate (%)		Total fertility rate			average annual rate of reduction (%)	
		1960	1980	1990	1960-80	1980-90	required** 1990-2000	1965-80	1980-89	1960	1980	1990	1960-80	1980-90
64	Ecuador	184	107	83	2.7	2.5	4.1	5.4	-0.5	6.9	5.1	4.1	1.5	2.2
65	Brazil	159	103	83	2.2	2.2	4.1	6.3	0.9	6.2	4.0	3.3	2.2	1.9
66	Papua New Guinea	248	112	80	4.0	3.4	4.1	. .	-0.7	6.3	5.7	5.0	0.5	1.3
67	Nicaragua	209	133	78	2.3	5.3	4.1	-0.7	-4.7ˣ	7.3	6.1	5.3	0.9	1.4
68	Dominican Rep.	199	103	78	3.3	2.8	4.1	3.8	-0.1	7.4	4.5	3.5	2.5	2.5
	Middle U5MR countries (21-70) Median	**134**	**53**	**35**	**4.5**	**3.7**	**4.1**	**3.7**	**-0.2**	**6.3**	**3.8**	**3.0**	**2.1**	**1.8**
69	Philippines	134	87	69	2.2	2.3	4.1	3.2	-1.8	6.9	4.9	4.1	1.7	1.8
70	Viet Nam	232	103	65	4.1	4.6	4.1	. .	. .	6.1	5.2	3.9	0.8	2.9
71	Tunisia	254	103	62	4.5	5.1	4.1	4.7	0.6	7.1	5.3	3.7	1.5	3.6
72	Paraguay	134	70	60	3.2	1.5	4.1	4.1	-1.5	6.8	4.9	4.5	1.6	0.9
73	Syria	217	88	59	4.5	4.0	4.1	5.1	-2.1	7.3	7.3	6.5	0.0	1.2
74	Iran, Islamic Rep. of	254	114	59	4.0	6.6	4.1	2.9	. .	7.2	5.8	5.0	1.1	1.5
75	Lebanon	91	62	56	1.9	1.0	4.1	. .	. .	6.3	4.0	3.6	2.3	1.1
76	Jordan	217	81	52	4.9	4.4	4.1	5.8ˣ	-3.0	7.7	7.1	5.8	0.4	2.0
77	Colombia	157	65	50	4.4	2.6	4.1	3.7	0.9	6.8	3.8	3.0	2.9	2.4
78	Mexico	140	68	49	3.6	3.3	4.1	3.6	-1.5	6.8	4.5	3.3	2.1	3.1
79	Oman	378	110	49	6.2	8.1	4.1	9.0	5.3	7.2	7.2	7.1	0.0	0.1
80	Venezuela	114	50	43	4.1	1.5	4.1	2.3	-2.3	6.5	4.3	3.6	2.1	1.8
81	China	203	56	42	6.4	2.9	4.1	4.1	8.2	5.7	2.6	2.4	3.9	0.8
82	Albania	151	57	37	4.9	4.3	4.1	. .	. .	5.9	3.8	2.9	2.2	2.7
83	Argentina	75	47	35	2.3	2.9	4.1	1.7	-1.6	3.1	3.3	2.9	-0.3	1.3
84	Korea, Dem.	120	44	35	5.0	2.3	4.1	. .	. .	5.7	3.1	2.5	3.0	2.2
85	Sri Lanka	114	53	35	3.8	4.1	4.1	2.8	2.4	5.3	3.5	2.6	2.1	3.0
86	Thailand	149	60	34	4.5	5.7	4.1	4.4	4.5	6.4	3.9	2.4	2.5	4.9
87	Romania	82	36	34	4.1	0.6	4.1	. .	. .	2.3	2.4	2.1	-0.2	1.3
88	USSR	53	37	31	1.8	1.8	4.1	. .	. .	2.7	2.3	2.3	0.8	0.0
89	Panama	105	43	31	4.5	3.3	4.1	2.8	-2.1	5.9	3.8	3.0	2.2	2.4
90	United Arab Emirates	239	43	30	8.6	3.6	4.1	. .	-8.2	6.9	5.4	4.6	1.2	1.6
91	Korea, Rep.	120	44	30	5.0	3.8	4.1	7.3	8.8	5.7	2.6	1.7	3.9	4.2
92	Malaysia	105	42	29	4.6	3.7	4.1	4.7	1.9	6.8	4.2	3.8	2.4	1.0
93	Mauritius	104	42	28	4.5	4.1	4.1	3.7	5.3	5.9	2.8	1.9	3.7	3.9
94	Chile	143	43	27	6.0	4.7	4.1	0.0	1.0	5.3	2.9	2.7	3.0	0.7
95	Uruguay	57	43	26	1.4	5.4	4.1	2.5	-0.8	2.9	2.7	2.4	0.4	1.2
96	Yugoslavia	113	37	23	5.6	4.8	4.1	5.2	-0.7	2.8	2.1	1.9	1.4	1.0
97	Costa Rica	121	31	22	6.8	3.4	4.1	3.3	0.4	7.0	3.7	3.1	3.2	1.8
	Low U5MR countries (20 and under) Median	**39**	**16**	**10**	**4.7**	**4.4**	**4.1**	**3.3**	**1.9**	**2.9**	**2.0**	**1.8**	**2.1**	**0.6**
98	Jamaica	89	28	20	5.8	3.4	4.1	-0.1	-1.7	5.4	3.8	2.5	1.8	4.2
99	Kuwait	128	34	19	6.6	5.8	4.1	0.6ˣ	-2.1	7.3	5.4	3.7	1.5	3.8
100	Poland	70	25	18	5.1	3.3	4.1	. .	1.8	3.0	2.3	2.2	1.3	0.4
101	Bulgaria	69	24	18	5.3	2.9	4.1	. .	. .	2.2	2.1	1.9	0.2	1.0
102	Trinidad and Tobago	67	26	17	4.7	4.2	4.1	3.1	-7.3	5.2	3.2	2.8	2.4	1.3
103	Hungary	57	26	16	3.9	4.9	4.1	5.1	1.4	2.0	2.0	1.8	0.0	1.1
104	Portugal	112	31	16	6.4	6.6	4.1	4.6	2.1	3.1	2.2	1.7	1.7	2.6
105	Cuba	87	25	14	6.2	5.8	4.1	. .	. .	4.2	2.0	1.9	3.7	0.5
106	Czechoslovakia	33	20	13	2.5	4.3	4.1	. .	. .	2.5	2.2	2.0	0.6	1.0
107	New Zealand	26	16	12	2.4	2.9	4.1	1.7	0.9	3.9	2.1	2.0	3.1	0.5
108	Israel	39	19	11	3.6	5.5	4.1	3.7	1.4	3.9	3.3	2.9	0.8	1.3
109	Greece	64	23	11	5.1	7.4	4.1	4.8	0.6	2.2	2.1	1.7	0.2	2.1
110	USA	29	15	11	3.3	3.1	4.1	1.8	2.2	3.5	1.9	1.8	3.1	0.5
111	Italy	50	18	10	5.1	5.9	4.1	3.2	2.1	2.5	1.7	1.4	1.9	1.9
112	Norway	22	10	10	3.9	0.0	4.1	3.6	3.5	2.9	1.8	1.7	2.4	0.6
113	Australia	24	13	10	3.1	2.6	4.1	2.2	1.8	3.3	2.0	1.8	2.5	1.1
114	Spain	57	16	10	6.4	4.7	4.1	4.1	2.4	2.8	2.2	1.6	1.2	3.2
115	Belgium	35	14	9	4.6	4.4	4.1	3.6	1.7	2.6	1.7	1.6	2.1	0.6
116	Austria	43	17	9	4.6	6.4	4.1	4.0	1.9	2.7	1.6	1.5	2.6	0.6
117	United Kingdom	27	15	9	2.9	5.1	4.1	2.0	2.9	2.7	1.8	1.8	2.0	0.0
118	Singapore	49	16	9	5.6	5.8	4.1	8.3	5.7	5.5	1.8	1.8	5.6	0.0
119	France	34	12	9	5.2	2.9	4.1	3.7	1.6	2.8	1.9	1.8	1.9	0.5
120	Switzerland	26	12	9	3.9	2.9	4.1	1.5	1.8	2.4	1.5	1.5	2.4	0.0
121	Denmark	25	10	9	4.6	1.1	4.1	2.2	2.2	2.6	1.5	1.5	2.4	0.0
122	Ireland	36	14	9	4.7	4.4	4.1	2.8	0.8	3.8	3.2	2.4	0.9	2.9
123	Germany	40	15	9	4.9	5.1	4.1	3.0ˣ	2.1ˣ	2.4	1.5	1.5	2.4	0.0
124	Canada	33	13	9	4.7	3.7	4.1	3.3	2.6	3.8	1.7	1.7	4.0	0.0
125	Netherlands	21	11	9	3.2	2.0	4.1	2.7	1.3	3.1	1.5	1.6	3.6	-0.6
126	Hong Kong	64	15	7	7.3	7.6	4.1	6.2	5.7	5.0	2.1	1.4	4.3	4.1
127	Finland	28	9	7	5.7	2.5	4.1	3.6	2.9	2.7	1.7	1.7	2.3	0.0
128	Sweden	20	9	7	4.0	2.5	4.1	2.0	2.0	2.3	1.7	1.9	1.5	-1.1
129	Japan	39	11	6	6.3	6.1	4.1	5.1	3.5	2.0	1.8	1.7	0.5	0.6

Footnotes to Tables

Table 1:
Basic
Indicators

Afghanistan	GNP per capita	1987
Belgium	Household income	1978-79
Bhutan	GNP per capita	1988
Cuba	GNP per capita	1987
France	Household income	1979
Germany	GNP per capita	Former Fed. Rep. of Germany only
	Household income	Former Fed. Rep. of Germany only
Iraq	GNP per capita	1987
Israel	Household income	1979
Japan	Household income	1979
Kenya	Household income	1976
Korea, Dem. Rep. of	GNP per capita	1987
Lebanon	GNP per capita	1987
Liberia	GNP per capita	1987
Mongolia	GNP per capita	1987
Myanmar	GNP per capita	1987
Nepal	Household income	1976-77
Nicaragua	GNP per capita	1987
Romania	GNP per capita	1990
Somalia	Adult literacy	1985
Sudan	GNP per capita	1988
Tanzania	Adult literacy	1986
Thailand	Household income	1976
Trinidad & Tobago	Household income	1976
USSR	GNP per capita	1980
United Kingdom	Household income	1979
Viet Nam	GNP per capita	1987
Yemen	Adult literacy	1985
Zambia	Household income	1976

Table 2:
Nutrition

Afghanistan	breastfeeding	Kabul only
	Calorie supply	1984-86
Albania	Calorie supply	1984-86
Algeria	Underweight	0-72 months
	Wasting	12-24 months
	Stunting	24-48 months
Australia	Low birth weight	1979
Bangladesh	breastfeeding	1975-76
	Underweight	6-59 months
Belgium	Calorie supply	1984-86
Bhutan	Underweight	0-60 months
	Wasting	0-60 months
	Stunting	0-60 months
Bolivia	Underweight	3-36 months
	Stunting	24-36 months
Botswana	Stunting	Clinic data
Brazil	breastfeeding	North-East only
Burkina Faso	Low birth weight	1979
Burundi	Low birth weight	Bujumbura only
	Underweight	3-36 months
	Stunting	24-36 months
Cambodia	Calorie supply	1984-86
Cameroon	Low birth weight	Yaounde only
	breastfeeding	1978
	Underweight	1978; 3-47 months
	Wasting	1978
	Stunting	1978; 24-47 months
Chile	Underweight	0-71 months
	Stunting	24-71 months
China	Underweight	9 provinces
	Wasting	9 provinces
	Stunting	9 provinces
Côte d'Ivoire	Low birth weight	1975; Abidjan only
Cuba	Wasting	Lowest 3 percentiles; 12-59 months
Djibouti	Wasting	0-59 months
Dominican Rep.	Underweight	6-36 months
	Stunting	24-36 months
Egypt	Underweight	3-36 months
	Stunting	24-36 months

continued over

Ethiopia	Underweight	Data from 9 zones
	Wasting	Data from 9 zones
	Stunting	Data from 9 zones
Finland	breastfeeding	1972
Guatemala	Underweight	3-36 months
	Stunting	24-36 months
Guinea-Bissau	Underweight	1978-80
Haiti	Low birth weight	1978
	Underweight	1978; Gomez; 3-59 months
	Wasting	1978
	Stunting	1978
Honduras	Wasting	0-59 months
	Stunting	0-59 months
India	Underweight	Gomez; 12-72 months; 8 States
Indonesia	Underweight	Moderate & severe <80% median
		Severe <60% median
Iran, Islamic Rep. of	Underweight	National rural
	Wasting	National rural
	Stunting	National rural
Jordan	Low birth weight	1979
Kenya	Stunting	National rural
	Wasting	National rural
Korea, Rep. of	breastfeeding	1978
Kuwait	breastfeeding	1978-79
Lao People's Dem. Rep.	breastfeeding	1979; 5 provinces only
Lesotho	breastfeeding	1977
Madagascar	Underweight	0-23 months
	Stunting	12-23 months
Malawi	Underweight	6-59 months
Mali	Underweight	3-36 months
	Stunting	24 36 months
Mauritania	Wasting	13-24 months
	Stunting	25-59 months
Mauritius	Wasting	0-59 months
	Stunting	0-59 months
Mexico	Wasting	0-59 months
	Stunting	0-59 months
Morocco	Underweight	0-36 months
	Stunting	24-36 months
Myanmar	Underweight	0-36 months
	Stunting	24-35 months
Namibia	breastfeeding	Northern areas
	Underweight	6-60 months; Northern areas
	Wasting	6-60 months; Northern areas
	Stunting	6-60 months; Northern areas
Nepal	breastfeeding	1976
Netherlands	breastfeeding	Excluding Amsterdam & Rotterdam
Niger	Wasting	0-59 months
	Stunting	0-59 months
Pakistan	Underweight	Gomez
	Wasting	<80% median; 13-24 months
	Stunting	<90% median; 25-60 months
Papua New Guinea	Low birth weight	1979
Peru	Underweight	0-71 months
Poland	breastfeeding	1977
Rwanda	Underweight	Mod. & severe <80% median; rural
		Severe <60% median; rural
	Wasting	<80% median; 13-24 months; rural
	Stunting	<90% median; 25-60 months; rural
Senegal	Underweight	6-36 months
	Stunting	24-36 months
Sierra Leone	Underweight	1977-78
	Wasting	1977-78
Singapore	Underweight	0-72 months
Sri Lanka	Underweight	3-36 months
	Stunting	24-36 months
Sudan	Wasting	0-59 months; Northern Sudan
	Stunting	0-59 months; Northern Sudan
Switzerland	Low birth weight	1979
Thailand	Underweight	3-36 months
	Stunting	24-36 months
Togo	Stunting	24-36 months
Trinidad and Tobago	Underweight	3-36 months
	Stunting	24-36 months

continued over

Tunisia	Underweight	3-36 months
	Stunting	24-36 months
USSR	Calorie supply	1984-86
Uganda	Stunting	24-60 months
Uruguay	Underweight	0-71 months
	Stunting	0-71 months
Venezuela	breastfeeding	1977
	Underweight	0-60 months
	Wasting	13-24 months
	Stunting	25-60 months
Viet Nam	Wasting	0-59 months; eight rural regions
	Stunting	0-59 months; eight rural regions
Yemen	breastfeeding	1979
	Underweight	1979-83; combined estimate
	Wasting	1979-83; combined estimate
	Stunting	1979-83; combined estimate
Zambia	Underweight	Rural only
	Wasting	Rural only
	Stunting	Rural only
Zimbabwe	Underweight	3-60 months
	Stunting	24-60 months

Gomez: moderate & severe - below 75% of median weight for age of reference population; severe - below 60% of median weight for age of reference population

Table 3:
Health

Algeria	Access to safe water	1985
Angola	Access to health services	1980
Austria	TB, DPT, Polio, Measles	1988
Botswana	Access to safe water	1985
	Access to health services	1980
Bulgaria	TB, DPT, Polio, Measles	1988
Burkina Faso	Access to health services	1980
Cambodia	Access to safe water	1985
Canada	DPT, Polio, Measles	1987-88
Costa Rica	Access to health services	1980
Côte d'Ivoire	Access to health services	1980
Egypt	Access to safe water	1985
Gabon	Access to health services	1983
Greece	DPT, Polio, Measles	1988
Hong Kong	Access to health services	1984
Israel	DPT, Polio, Measles	1988
Italy	DPT	DT only
Kenya	Access to safe water	1985
Liberia	TB, DPT, Polio, Measles, Tetanus	1988
Malawi	Access to safe water	1985
New Zealand	TB, DPT, Polio, Measles	1987-88
Panama	Access to health services	1980
Paraguay	Access to health services	1980
Peru	Access to health services	1980
Rwanda	Access to safe water	1985
	Access to health services	1980
Senegal	Access to safe water	1985
Somalia	Access to health services	1980
Spain	DPT, Polio, Measles	1988
Sri Lanka	Access to health services	1980
Sweden	TB, Polio, Measles	1988
	DPT	1988; DT only
Syrian Arab Rep.	Access to health services	1980
Tanzania	Access to health services	1980
Trinidad and Tobago	Access to safe water	1985
Tunisia	Access to health services	1983
Turkey	Access to safe water	1985
USA	DPT, Polio, Measles	1988
Uganda	Access to health services	1980
United Arab Emirates	Access to health services	1980
Venezuela	Access to safe water	1985
Yemen	Access to safe water	Northern 80% of country
Yugoslavia	TB, DPT, Polio, Measles	1988
Zambia	Access to health services	1980

continued over

Table 4:
Education

Belgium	Radio sets	Licences only
	TV sets	Licences only
Bulgaria	Radio sets	Licences only
	TV sets	Licences only
Czechoslovakia	Radio sets	Licences only
Denmark	Radio sets	Licences only
Germany	TV sets	Licences only
Greece	TV sets	Licences only
Haiti	Adult literacy (1970)	1971
Hong Kong	Adult literacy (1970)	1971
	Reaching final grade	1980
India	TV sets	Licences only
Lebanon	Adult literacy (1970)	Age 10 years and older
Mauritius	Radio sets	Licences only
	TV sets	Licences only
Morocco	TV sets	Licences only
Norway	TV sets	Licences only
Pakistan	Reaching final grade	1981
Paraguay	Adult literacy (1970)	1972
Poland	Radio sets	Licences only
	TV sets	Licences only
Portugal	TV sets	Licences only
Romania	TV sets	Licences only
Singapore	Radio sets	Licences only
Somalia	Adult literacy	1985
Sudan	Primary enrolment	1985
Sweden	TV sets	Licences only
Switzerland	Radio sets	Licences only
Tanzania	Adult literacy	1986
Uruguay	Adult literacy (1970)	1975
Yemen	Adult literacy	1985
	Reaching final grade	1983
Yugoslavia	Radio sets	Licences only
	TV sets	Licences only

Table 6:
Economic
Indicators

Afghanistan	GNP per capita	1987
	Poverty level	1977
Algeria	Poverty level	1977
Bangladesh	Poverty level	1976 77
Bhutan	GNP per capita	1988
	GNP per capita growth rate	1980-88
Botswana	GNP per capita growth rate	1980-88
Burundi	Poverty level	1978
Cameroon	Poverty level	1979
Chad	Poverty level	1976
Chile	Debt service	1988
Cuba	GNP per capita	1987
Dominican Republic	Poverty level	1978
Egypt	GNP per capita growth rate	1980-88
Germany	GNP per capita	Former Fed. Rep. of Germany only
	GNP per capita growth rate	Former Fed. Rep. of Germany only
	Inflation rate	Former Fed. Rep. of Germany only
Greece	Debt service	1988
Hungary	Debt service	1988
India	Debt service	1988
Iraq	GNP per capita	1987
	Inflation rate	1980-87
Jordan	GNP per capita growth rate	1970-80
	Inflation rate	1980-88
	Poverty level	1977
Kenya	Poverty level	1977
Korea, Dem. Rep. of	GNP per capita	1987
Korea, Rep.	Poverty level	1978
Kuwait	GNP per capita growth rate	1965-86
Laos	GNP per capita growth rate	1980-88
Lebanon	GNP per capita	1987
Lesotho	Poverty level	1979
Liberia	GNP per capita	1987
	GNP per capita growth rate	1980-88
	Poverty level	1977

continued over

Libya	GNP per capita growth rate	1980-88
Madagascar	Poverty level	1977
Mali	GNP per capita growth rate	1967-80
	Poverty level	1975
Mauritius	Poverty level	1979
Mongolia	GNP per capita	1987
Morocco	Poverty level	1979
Myanmar	GNP per capita	1987
	Poverty level	1978
Nepal	Poverty level	1979
Nicaragua	GNP per capita	1987
	GNP per capita growth rate	1980-88
	Inflation rate	1980-88
	Poverty level	1977
Niger	Poverty level	1978
Pakistan	Poverty level	1979
Panama	Poverty level	1978
Papua New Guinea	Poverty level	1979
Paraguay	Poverty level	1978
Romania	GNP per capita	1990
	Debt service	1988
Rwanda	Poverty level	1977
Saudi Arabia	GNP per capita growth rate	1965-86
Sierra Leone	Poverty level	1977
	Debt service	1988
Somalia	Poverty level	1978
Sudan	GNP per capita	1988
	GNP per capita growth rate	1980-88
	Inflation rate	1980-88
	Poverty level	1975
Syria	Debt service	1988
Togo	Poverty level	1978
Trinidad & Tobago	Poverty level	1977
Tunisia	Poverty level	1977
USSR	GNP per capita	1980
Viet Nam	GNP per capita	1987
Zaire	Poverty level	1975

Table 7:
Women

Afghanistan	Contraceptive prevalence	1976
Algeria	Contraceptive prevalence	1977
	Maternal mortality	1978
Angola	Contraceptive prevalence	1977
Australia	Contraceptive prevalence	1970
	Births attended	1982
Austria	Contraceptive prevalence	Marriage cohorts of 1974 & 1978
Belgium	Contraceptive prevalence	Flemish population
Benin	Maternal mortality	Hospital data only
Bulgaria	Contraceptive prevalence	1976
Cameroon	Contraceptive prevalence	1978
Chad	Contraceptive prevalence	1977
	Births attended	1980-82
Chile	Contraceptive prevalence	1978
China	Maternal mortality	30 provinces
Czechoslovakia	Contraceptive prevalence	1977; ever used while married
Denmark	Births attended	1979
Finland	Contraceptive prevalence	1977
	Births attended	1979
France	Contraceptive prevalence	1978
	Births attended	1976
Germany	Births attended	1977-79
Greece	Births attended	1978
Guinea	Contraceptive prevalence	1977
	Maternal mortality	Hospital data only
Hungary	Births attended	1982
Iran	Contraceptive prevalence	1978
Italy	Contraceptive prevalence	1979; since last pregnancy
Jordan	Maternal mortality	1979, hospital data only
Kenya	Maternal mortality	1977
Lesotho	Contraceptive prevalence	1977

continued over

Liberia	Tetanus	1988
Libyan Arab Jamahiriya	Maternal mortality	1978
Morocco	Births attended	1980
	Maternal mortality	1974
Namibia	Maternal mortality	Northern areas only.
Netherlands	Births attended	1978
New Zealand	Contraceptive prevalence	1976
Nicaragua	Births attended	Institutional deliveries only
Niger	Contraceptive prevalence	1977
Nigeria	Births attended	1980
Norway	Contraceptive prevalence	1977; during past 4 weeks
Poland	Contraceptive prevalence	1977
	Births attended	1980
Portugal	Contraceptive prevalence	1979
	Births attended	1978
Romania	Contraceptive prevalence	1978
	Births attended	1979
Rwanda	Maternal mortality	All hospitals
Somalia	Adult literacy	1985
South Africa	Maternal mortality	From 267 hospitals
Sudan	Primary enrolment	1985
Sweden	Births attended	1976
Switzerland	Contraceptive prevalence	Marriage cohorts of 1970-79
	Births attended	1976
Syrian Arab Rep.	Contraceptive prevalence	1978
Tanzania	Adult literacy	1986
	Contraceptive prevalence	1977
	Maternal mortality	From 48 hospitals; all regions
United Kingdom	Births attended	1978
Uruguay	Births attended	Institutional deliveries only
Venezuela	Contraceptive prevalence	1977
Yemen	Adult literacy	1985
Yugoslavia	Contraceptive prevalence	1976; during last 6 months
	Births attended	1979
Zaire	Contraceptive prevalence	1977
Zambia	Contraceptive prevalence	1977

Table 8:

Basic Indicators on less populous countries

Antigua	GNP per capita	1988
Bahamas	Adult literacy	1981
Bahrain	GNP per capita	1988
Barbados	Primary enrolment	1984
British Virgin Islands	GNP per capita	1983
	Life expectancy	1980
	Adult literacy	1970
Brunei Darussalam	GNP per capita	1987
	Adult literacy	1981
	Measles	1988
Cape Verde	Adult literacy	1970; aged 14 and over
Comoros	Adult literacy	1980
Cook Islands	GNP per capita	1987
Cyprus	Adult literacy	1976
Djibouti	GNP per capita	1987
Dominica	GNP per capita	1988
	Adult literacy	1970
Equatorial Guinea	Primary enrolment	1983
Fed.States of Micronesia	Adult literacy	1982
	Primary enrolment	1982
Fiji	Adult literacy	1976
Grenada	Adult literacy	1984
	Primary enrolment	1984
Guyana	Adult literacy	1970
Kiribati	Primary enrolment	1985
Luxembourg	Measles	1988
Marshall Islands	Adult literacy	1982
	Measles	1988
Montserrat	GNP per capita	1987
	Adult literacy	1970
	Primary enrolment	1982
Palau	GNP per capita	1986
	Primary enrolment	1982

continued over

Saint Lucia	Adult literacy	1970
	Primary enrolment	1980
Saint Vincent	GNP per capita	1988
	Primary enrolment	1982
Samoa	Primary enrolment	1985
Sao Tome and Principe	Adult literacy	1981
Seychelles	Primary enrolment	1982
Solomon Islands	Primary enrolment	1983
St. Christopher-Nevis	GNP per capita	1988
Swaziland	Adult literacy	1976
Tonga	Primary enrolment	1984
Turks & Caicos Islands	GNP per capita	1987
	Adult literacy	1970
Tuvalu	Infant mortality rate	1985
	GNP per capita	1987
Vanuatu	Adult literacy	1979
	Primary enrolment	1984

Table 9:
The
rate of
progress

Bhutan	GNP per capita growth rate	1980-88
Botswana	GNP per capita growth rate	1980-88
Egypt	GNP per capita growth rate	1980-88
Germany	GNP per capita growth rate	Former Fed. Rep. of Germany only
Jordan	GNP per capita growth rate	1970-80
Kuwait	GNP per capita growth rate	1965-86
Laos	GNP per capita growth rate	1980-88
Liberia	GNP per capita growth rate	1980-88
Libya	GNP per capita growth rate	1980-88
Mali	GNP per capita growth rate	1967-80
Nicaragua	GNP per capita growth rate	1980-88
Saudi Arabia	GNP per capita growth rate	1965-86
Sudan	GNP per capita growth rate	1980-88

Definitions

Under five mortality rate: annual number of deaths of children under five years of age per 1,000 live births. More specifically this is the probability of dying between birth and exactly five years of age.

Infant mortality rate: annual number of deaths of infants under one year of age per 1,000 live births. More specifically this is the probability of dying between birth and exactly one year of age.

GNP: gross national product. Annual GNP's per capita are expressed in current United States dollars. GNP per capita growth rates are average annual growth rates that have been computed by fitting trend lines to the logarithmic values of GNP per capita at constant market prices for each year of the time period.

Life expectancy at birth: the number of years new-born children would live if subject to the mortality risks prevailing for the cross-section of population at the time of their birth.

Adult literacy rate: percentage of persons aged 15 and over who can read and write.

Primary and secondary enrolment ratios: the gross enrolment ratio is the total number of children enrolled in a schooling level - whether or not they belong in the relevant age group for that level - expressed as a percentage of the total number of children in the relevant age group for that level. The net enrolment ratio is the total number of children enrolled in a schooling level who belong in the relevant age group, expressed as a percentage of the total number in that age group.

Income share: percentage of private income received by the highest 20% and lowest 40% of households.

Low birth weight: less than 2,500 grammes.

Breast-feeding: percentage of mothers either wholly or partly breastfeeding.

Underweight: *moderate and severe* - below minus two standard deviations from median weight for age of reference population;

severe - below minus three standard deviations from median weight for age of reference population.

Wasting: *moderate and severe* - below minus two standard deviations from median weight for height of reference population.

Stunting: *moderate and severe* - below minus two standard deviations from median height for age of reference population.

Access to health services: percentage of the population that can reach appropriate local health services by the local means of transport in no more than one hour.

DPT: diphtheria, pertussis (whooping cough) and tetanus.

ORT use: percentage of all cases of diarrhoea in children under five years of age treated with oral rehydration salts or an appropriate household solution.

Children reaching final grade of primary school: percentage of the children entering the first grade of primary school who eventually reach the final grade.

Crude death rate: annual number of deaths per 1,000 population.

Crude birth rate: annual number of births per 1,000 population.

Total fertility rate: the number of children that would be born per woman, if she were to live to the end of her child-bearing years and bear children at each age in accordance with prevailing age-specific fertility rates.

Urban population: percentage of population living in urban areas as defined according to the national definition used in the most recent population census.

Absolute poverty level: the income level below which a minimum nutritionally adequate diet plus essential non-food requirements is not affordable.

ODA: official development assistance.

Debt service: the sum of interest payments and repayments of principal on external public and publicly guaranteed long-term debts.

Contraceptive prevalence: percentage of married women age 15-49 currently using contraception.

Births attended: percentage of births attended by physicians, nurses, midwives, trained primary health care workers or trained traditional birth attendants.

Maternal mortality rate: annual number of deaths of women from pregnancy related causes per 100,000 live births.

Main sources

Under five and infant mortality:	United Nations Population Division, UNICEF, United Nations Statistical Office and World Bank.
Total population:	United Nations Population Division.
Births:	United Nations Population Division, United Nations Statistical Office and World Bank.
Under five deaths:	United Nations Population Division and UNICEF.
GNP per capita:	World Bank.
Life expectancy:	United Nations Population Division.
Adult literacy:	United Nations Educational, Scientific and Cultural Organization (UNESCO).
School enrolment and completion:	United Nations Educational, Scientific and Cultural Organization (UNESCO).
Household Income:	World Bank.
Low birth-weight:	World Health Organization (WHO).
Breast-feeding:	World Health Organization (WHO).
Underweight, wasting and stunting:	World Health Organization (WHO) and Demographic and Health Surveys, IRD.
Food production and calorie intake:	Food and Agricultural Organization of the United Nations (FAO).
Income spent on food:	World Bank.
Access to drinking water:	World Health Organization (WHO) and UNICEF.

Access to health services:	UNICEF.
Immunization:	World Health Organization (WHO) and UNICEF.
ORT use:	World Health Organization (WHO).
Radio and television:	United Nations Educational, Scientific and Cultural Organization (UNESCO).
Child population:	United Nations Population Division.
Crude death and birth rates:	United Nations Population Division.
Fertility:	United Nations Population Division.
Urban population:	United Nations Population Division.
Inflation and absolute poverty level:	World Bank.
Expense on health, education and defense:	World Bank and International Monetary Fund (IMF).
ODA:	Organisation for Economic Co-operation and Development (OECD).
Debt service:	World Bank.
Contraceptive prevalence:	United Nations Population Division, Rockefeller Foundation and Demographic and Health Surveys, IRD.
Births attended:	World Health Organization (WHO).
Maternal mortality:	World Health Organization (WHO).

UNICEF Headquarters
UNICEF House, 3 UN Plaza, New York, NY 10017, USA

UNICEF Geneva Office
Palais des Nations, CH-1211 Geneva 10, Switzerland

UNICEF Regional Office for Eastern and Southern Africa
P.O. Box 44145, Nairobi, Kenya

UNICEF Regional Office for Central and West Africa
P.O. Box 443, Abidjan 04, Côte d'Ivoire

UNICEF Regional Office for the Americas and the Caribbean
Apartado Aéreo 75 55, Bogotá, Colombia

UNICEF Regional Office for East Asia and Pakistan
P.O. Box 2-154, Bangkok 10200, Thailand

UNICEF Regional Office for the Middle East and North Africa
P.O. Box 811721, Amman, Jordan

UNICEF Regional Office for South Central Asia
UNICEF House, 73 Lodi Estate, New Delhi 110003, India

UNICEF Office for Australia and New Zealand
P.O. Box Q143, Queen Victoria Building, Sydney,
N.S.W. 2000, Australia

UNICEF Office for Japan
22nd floor Shin-Aoyama Building Nishikan
1-1, Minami-Aoyama, 1-Chome, Minato-Ku, Tokyo 107, Japan